THE ISRAEL I LOVE

NOEL CALEF

THE
I S R A E L
I LOVE

Foreword
JOSEPH KESSEL

Photographer
DAVID HARRIS

General Editor
MORDECAI RAANAN

Captions
JUDITH LELYVELD

LEON AMIEL PUBLISHER

Translated from French by
Ruth Whipple FERMAUD

Copyright © 1977 by NATEEV Ltd. P.O.Box 6048, Tel-Aviv, Israel

ACKNOWLEDGMENTS and thanks are due to the following persons for having
kindly permitted the use of their photographs: Yael Braun — pages 13, 16, 17, 20, 21,
25, 37, 40, 42, 43, 46, 47, 80, 82, 85, 109, 117, 128, 142; Haifa University—page 33;
Azaria Allon — pages 53, 114: Shimon Fuchs — page 75; Nuri Fisher — page 136.

Printed in Israel by Peli Printing Works Ltd.

FOREWORD

I was lying in the sea in Elath under a very light wave, gentle, silky, and living. This sort of liquid scarf was a necessity, for although it was springtime the sun burned without mercy.

On my right the Sinai desert began. On the left at the far end of the gulf, fitting together to form a single block, the Arab houses of the port of Aqaba. And that was Jordan. Opposite, on the other side of the water, sand waves undulated. And that was Saudi Arabia.

A breeze coming from the north ruffled the surface of land and sea. It had the gentleness of a caress, the coolness of paradise. It was as regular, as constant as the flow and song of a brook. It is said—tradition, legend, history?—that its breath in Biblical times stirred like a forge bellows the fires in King Solomon's coppermines.

The same mines where, after so many centuries, live coals again were glowing . . .

A young girl came out of the sea and lay down not far from me. Her hair was a pure, pale blond and her skin extraordinarily fine-grained and delicate. I saw her several times a day. She was working as a waitress in the restaurant of my hotel. A dark, thin man came to stretch out beside her and began a conversation in English. He had a very pronounced Central European accent. Hers, in contrast, was perfect in ease, precision and trueness. He was amazed. She replied laughingly.

"No wonder. My father was a sergeant in the British army here during the war. He met my mother and married her. After the war he returned to his regular job: mining. I was born and grew up in England."

"And then?" asked the man.

"My mother was homesick," the girl answered. "It so happened that specialists were needed for King Solomon's mines which had just been reopened. So, one mine being as good as another, you see . . ."

"Yes, I see," he answered.

Before going into the water he took off his watch. This gesture revealed, above the wrist, a number tattooed in blue-black ink . . . A number received in one of the concentration camps.

The former deportee put on a diving mask and swam to the place where the depths offer their most fabulous spectacle.

On the same coast a large Israeli fishing boat, half ship, half factory, unloaded cases sparkling with frost and filled with fish caught in the Red Sea along the Ethiopian coast.

Aside from that, Elath, with its new hotels, its entertainment, its games, its tourists arriving each day in private cars, buses and planes, was a vacation beach like many others throughout the world.

The old man whom I saw the next day at the other end of Israel on the banks of the Jordan was very much like other men who tilled the soil and who, after a long, patient and laborious existence, dream on their doorstep and smile at their guest.

And yet . . .

This one had left the Ukraine at the beginning of the century, reached Palestine while it was still a province of the Ottoman Empire and, in 1911, with a few other pioneers of the old, heroic days, had joined forces, in spite of swamps, malaria, dysentery, and stark poverty, to found the first of those admirable communities which, since then, have become famous under the name of kibbutzim.

When I visited him magnificent cypress trees and majestic eucalypti surrounded Deganya. The orchards were richly laden and the gardens fragrant. The song of countless birds rose in the air like a hymn of joy. Everything—the man, his house, his village, gave an impression of peace, security, happiness, and almost of eternity.

And yet . . .

It had been necessary, in pestilence and fever, to build stone by stone, to clear and drain the land inch by inch, to plant tree by tree. They had had to work, work and above all believe, in spite of obstacles, in spite of the odds against them, in spite of common sense, believe with every fiber, with every breath. They had had to survive two world wars and then fight a third against six Arab countries at a time when Israel was just a newborn nation numbering scarcely 600,000 inhabitants and unarmed, at that.

Deganya was less than a mile from the frontier and commanded the approach to Galilee and Haifa. The Syrian army attacked in full force with artillery and tanks. To defend the kibbutz there were only the settlers with a motley assortment of rifles. How could those men and women repel an enemy so overwhelmingly superior in number and means? The exploit belongs to that chain of miracles taking place at that same time on the fronts of Galilee, Jerusalem, Lebanon, and the Negev against the soldiers of Egypt and Iraq, the Saudi Arabian warriors, and the Legion of Jordan formed, officered and armed by the English.

When one walks in the springtime in the large and marvelous garden that separates the two sections of the Deganya kibbutz, one sees a half-buried tank on which a shower of petals falls. It is a Syrian tank. In May, 1948, it had crossed the canal and road, crushing, uprooting trees, killing whatever lay in its path. At that moment one of the boys from the kibbutz, a former guerrilla soldier from Leningrad, had jumped in front of it and, with a Molotov cocktail of his own making, set fire to the iron monster.

During those combats the old man who sat smiling at me in front of his flower-bedecked house had been responsible for his village on the Jordan.

Another old man received me a few days later. He, too, was friendly and simple. He, too, had left Russia at the turn of the century and had modeled his whole existence around making a dream come true, a utopia, a chimera, a mad fancy. But he, in the crucial years, was responsible not only for a kibbutz but for the whole of Israel. Yes, I had before me David Ben-Gurion, government leader, war leader.

The meeting took place near Tel Aviv in a hotel by the sea where Ben-Gurion was taking a few hours' rest. There was no ostentation or ceremony. The years of poverty, of labor, of peril, the trials of an arduous life in common with other men, had marked Ben-Gurion forever with a direct and slightly brusque familiarity which recalls that of old peasants, old shepherds, or sailors.

While he — in his shirtsleeves, the open collar revealing his muscular neck, his face deeply tanned and etched under an abundant head of white hair — sipped his tea, I mused on the extraordinary and marvelous destiny of that man.

He was one of the major artisans in transmuting into land, flesh and blood the dream of a dispersed people, proscribed and hunted for two millenaries. He had lived, he had built, he had directed the unbelievable, the impossible adventure step by step: Turkish province, British mandate, State of Israel. And at its completion that adventure was incarnated in him. He was governing the most ancient and youngest nation in the world, which had relearned the language of the prophets and which was composed of people coming from over one hundred different countries, some belonging to the most advanced civilisations and others to Biblical tradition.

I asked Ben-Gurion: "What, for you, was the greatest moment in your life?"

Ben-Gurion, running his hand through his leonine mop of hair and tousling it, reflected.

"Perhaps the return of the Jews of Yemen. They had lived there for centuries and centuries, penned in ghettos, enslaved, despised, exploited by the warriors of Arabia Felix. They submitted to it all with serenity. Because they believed with a simple and ardent faith in the prophecy of the eagle. It declared that a royal, giant-sized bird would one day descend from the sky to deliver them from their condition, from shame, and carry them back to the land of their ancestors. And the eagle, as it had been promised, came.

"Undoubtedly, for you and for me, it was only an obsolete plane, the first of those which our government, after an agreement with the imam of San'a, chartered and, in an amazing operation, repatriated all the Jews of Yemen. But for them who had never seen a flying machine it was purely and simply the Promise fulfilled.

"I was the airport to greet them . . . The way those lost children kissed the Israeli soil . . . the rapture in their eyes . . . the music in their words . . . Yes, I think that is my greatest memory . . ."

I then asked: "And the most painful?"

This time Ben-Gurion did not hesitate: "When we had to return Mount Sinai," he said. His voice became curt, his face gaunt.

"It was after the Suez campaign," he continued. "We had reached the Canal, won considerable territory. And then, by a decision of the United Nations, we had to return to our former boundaries. Our soldiers, without revolting, abandoned all the terrain they had taken. All . . . except the Sinai. For them it was Moses . . . the Decalogue . . . I had to rush out there to explain, plead, threaten, beg. The rabbi chaplains insulted me, cursed me . . . The tank drivers, the parachutists cried . . . When I had finally convinced them, believe me, I wasn't proud of myself . . . Everyone knows it: I've always been an atheist . . . But . . . the Bible . . . and Mount Sinai . . ."

If, by way of a preface to this book and its photographs, which are the best invitation to know Israel, I have told a few brief stories, it is to try to make the reader sense on what depths of events, hopes, deeds, pain and marvels reposes everything that meets the eye in this most amazing of countries. The desert as well as the orange plantations, the kibbutz as well as the large city. August ruins and the visage of daily life.

This cab driver was one of the Mount Sinai parachutists. This Yemenite farmer arrived on the prophet's eagle. And the men who bear on their wrists a death camp tattoo are so common on the beach in good weather that one scarcely notices them.

Josef KESSEL

8

A land so narrow that a man can walk across it during a day's hike in the north, in the south, and in the center. As for its length, from Metulla on the northern border to the port of Elath on the Red Sea, wedged between Egypt and Jordan, the distance is less than three hundred miles, approximately that between New York and Pittsburgh.

A nation at war since its creation; an economic development which must support the burden of the longest known armistice—with the exception of the interruptions in the Hundred Years War. A Jewish population smaller than that of the Jews in New York alone. An independence proclaimed in a house on Rothschild Boulevard in Tel Aviv, in the name of 600,000 men, women, children and old people who declared themselves free at last. Free, while 40 million enemies were crossing their borders, swearing to exterminate them once again. A few more than three-and-a-half million inhabitants today, coming from the four corners of the earth, from 102 different countries; 103 now, if one counts the generation born in Israel and now reaching maturity.

Israel. A wondrous land from which its people were dispersed and reviled without discrimination everywhere for 2,000 years.

A heteroclite people forever arguing among themselves, yet so fiercely united and interdependent that they resisted dispersion and persecution for 1878 years (1948, birth of Israel—70, destruction of the Temple), to be born again in the face of storm, tide and politics, reviving a dead language, which was Hebrew, for all. Prodigious workers, more alive and active than ever, after concentration camps and death, after wandering and exile, deportation and massacre.

"If I were to tell my life story, sir, they'd write a book about it."

It has been written. It was written before the existence of any literary fashion: the Bible. (From *Biblia*, neuter plural, meaning "the books.") Translated one hundred times if not more. The first Western edition, the Greek, dates from 283 A.D., the *Septuagint*, the work of the *Septante*, seventy, who, in actual fact, were seventy-two. In the follow-

ing century the man who was later to become the patron saint of translators, Saint Jerome, personally assumed the task. Later, much later, the Greek text was retranslated into Latin. This new version was called the *Vulgate*. The Catholic Church adopted it during the Council of Trent.

It has become a best-seller.

In the beginning we are told of the Creation. The works of the Creator are divided into days: "And there was evening and there was morning, one day." How long did those evenings and days last? That's a good question when one discovers that the average age of the first seven patriarchs was 700 years! That would make seven millenaries up to the Flood: 3926 B.C., in principle. The Jewish calendar, which starts on "the first day" is now in the year 5737. Scholars juggle with hundreds of thousands, even millions of years. It's true that God did not give us the Sun and the Moon until the fourth day, which allowed us to establish the rule of 24 hours. Even in the last century there was none of our present day concern for exactitude. Some scholars spoke matter-of-factly

of the year I of the Creation. Cain was born in II, Abel in III. The famous murder took place in 129. There was no question of their being mistaken, but they were, nonetheless, modest enough to add that these dates were conjectural.

So where are we? One gets lost in the labyrinth of numbers. It doesn't really matter. Archaic imagery is more memorable to us than the precisions of carbon 14. We prefer an Adam moulded from the clay of the earth, an Eve fashioned from a rib taken from her husband's side, to the *homo sapiens* who matured so slowly in the sun after evolving from the coelenterate fish, and the anthropoid ape. In any case, believers will continue to ask the insidious and futile question, "Which came first, the chicken or the egg?".

The fact remains that because of certain practices displeasing to the Creator, Adam and Eve were banished from Eden. Scholars situate this earthly Paradise hypothetically between the Tigris and the Euphrates in Asia Minor. As the first couple was leaving the Garden of Eden, in disgrace, an angel of fire pointed his sword to indicate the direction

12

A breathtaking view from Margalioth in Upper Galilee: the mighty mountain mass of Mount Hermon looming over the Huleh Valley, at the northern end of the Golan Heights. Its 7,500 feet high, snow-capped head is visible all over Galilee, while its cool breeze during the hot summer months is especially appreciated.

they were to go: West. This is the road of civilizations and that is how the history of humanity begins. That of the Jews as well.

Today our time measure is based on a birth. Modern history distinguishes between before Christ, B. C., and after, A. D., *anno domini*. There's no risk of confusion. Each year we progress one unit. For "before" we subtract one, counting backwards. Nothing is to prevent us from one day saying, "Such and such an event took place in the year 14845729 B. C. And the date will no longer be conjectural.

It is by chronological approximation that ethnologists and historians on the one hand, and computers on the other, have reached an agreement. One day God invited Abraham to leave Ur in Chaldea (a Babylonian region) and go to the land of Canaan where "milk and honey" flowed. This departure coincides with the passage of homo sapiens from the nomadic state to the sedentary. Man thus entered the neolithic age. This is a scientific notion which is impossible to determine with exactitude. The transformation of our an-

A recreational park in the Huleh Valley at the foot of the Hermon, the Tal Grove of massive ancient oaks, its spacious well-tended lawns crisscrossed by the icy streams of the Dan river, is a beauty spot beloved by all, old and young. The streams gather into a delightful, natural swimming-pool, flowing out of it again to join two other rivulets—the Banias and the Hatzbani—which form together the Jordan River.

cestors' mode of existence was dependent upon climate, the degree of technical progress attained, the thinking process—factors as numerous as they are diverse. At the present time tribes exist on our planet which have not yet taken the hurdle. They still live by hunting, moving on foot, seeking pasture lands for their herds, going elsewhere when the grass is gone; they know nothing of the joys of a permanent residence, oil or gas heating, chemical fertilizer, or hybrid corn. Our past is very likely to be their future.

However, theory and legend agree on this point: with Abraham the elected people went West. The nomads settled. We can't be sure that the wheel had been invented but we can affirm that they carried with them a revolutionary new concept which was to transform the human spirit: that of a unique God. Monotheism. Those people were the ancestors of the Jews. And Canaan, the land where milk and honey flowed, was Sinai. Palestine. Israel.

Nowadays it seems that all roads lead to Rome. Once upon a time they led to Jerusalem, which was called *Salem*. It is said that

Once an extensive swamp where the malaria-carrying anopheles mosquito reigned supreme, the Huleh valley has been turned in the past twenty five years into prime agricultural land. The waters of the Jordan river which constituted the lake and marshes of the Huleh have been drained into channels, flowing southward into the Kinnereth. Part of the Huleh Lake has been left intact as a nature reserve, to preserve its rich and varied vegetation and wildlife. The reserve, teeming with migrant birds in winter months, among them the charming pelicans and storks, is a birdswatcher's paradise.

Fishponds in the Huleh Valley yield rich catches of silver carp and St. Peter's fish. The formerly malaria infested and thus shunned by people valley is presently extensively cultivated by the many kibbutzim that settled on its drained fertile soil.

Safed, artists' quarter. The decrepit old stone houses and narrow twisting alleys had an irresistible appeal to many of Israel's painters and sculptors in their search of the picturesque and off-beat. Restored by the artists themselves, the cen- turies-old crumbling houses, the immaculately tidy lanes and countless art galleries form the charming quarter which draws hundreds of visitors, vacationers and tourists.

Situated on a mountaintop, like an eagle's nest, Safed has enjoyed a well-deserved renown not only for its magnificent setting and refreshingly cool climate; one of Judaism's four holy cities (the other three are Jerusalem, Hebron and Tiberias) it was the center of the Cabbalists and great rabbinical scholars since the 15th century, and the vast Jewish cemetery covering an entire mountainslope testifies to an almost uninterrupted Jewish habitation during the past eighteen centuries.

its king, Melchizedek, blessed Abraham on his arrival and offered him "bread and wine." Wine. Consequently the migration took place after the Deluge. Some wizards claim that Abraham set out in 1910 B.C. How can we verify that?

On the other hand, there *is* a continuity apparent in the age of the patriarch. He was 75 years old when he left Ur. He was 86 "after spending 10 years" in his new residence, when an incident occurred. His wife, Sarah, sterile and no longer young, despaired of giving him an heir and so offered him the pretty slave Hagar as a bed companion. Wives in those days were extremely considerate. From this union Ishmael was born.

Shortly thereafter, an angel came to Sarah and announced that she, too, would conceive. In spite of her age she gave birth to Isaac.

Did Sarah fear that Ishmael, born of a slave, would offend Isaac, the legitimate son? Did she experience belated jealousy? Whatever the reason, she drove out Hagar and Ishmael.

An angel appeared before the poor wan-

On the shores of the enchanting Lake of Galilee lies Tiberias, the town which has been an integral part of the history of the Jewish people for the past twenty centuries, and one of its four holy cities. Its ancient cemetery contains the tombs of great rabbinical scholars and philosophers; especially revered are the tombs of Rabbi Akiba, one of greatest intellectuals of his day, who supported the Bar Kochba revolt in the 3rd century, and of the famous Rambam, known to the western world by his name of Maimonides. In the foreground is the tomb of rabbi Meir the Miracle Maker, and next to it a complex of *yeshivoth* (rabbinical colleges) and students' quarters. One of the town's main sources of income is fishing. The lake yields rich catches of fish, especially the highly appreciated St. Peter's fish.

derers in the desert and directed them to Egypt, the native land of the beautiful Hagar. Ishmael later took a wife there and had twelve sons whose families became the twelve Arab tribes. Later Mohammed was to pride himself on descending from Ishmael. For a long time the Arabs were called Ishmaelites. (Not to be confused with Ismailians, a sect issuing from a relatively recent Islamic branch whose spiritual leader is the Aga Khan).

Isaac grew. His parents undoubtedly spoiled him, the only child of an old couple. The Eternal Father knew that this son was the apple of Abraham's eye. To test him, He commanded the old man to sacrifice the boy. Heartsick, the patriarch was about to obey when an angel stayed his raised hand.

The scene took place on *The Rock*. In the Middle Ages map-makers considered that rock the key to the mystery of the Universe and drew the Earth around it. The rock still exists, in Jerusalem. The Mosque of Omar stands on the site of Abraham's sacrifice in the city holy to three great monotheistic communities — Christendom, Islam and Israel.

Slowly legend and revelation became a part of History about two thousand years B.C. From Abraham, who led his people into the neolithic so dear to our scholars, came forth Jews, Christians, and Moslems. In that order.

We have read the Bible. We have conserved an impression of nostalgic charm and a few mental images. What has impressed us, what we have retained is the anecdote. History with a capital H is fixed in our memory by little stories. They have also inspired the poet, the painter, the sculptor and, more recently, the film producer. The rest of us look at religious pictures, idealized by the artist, with the pleasure of the initiated. Citations in great and less great literature, paintings on museum walls, an opera and its music, a film by the late Cecil B. de Mille, have all familiarized us with the general trend of past events. Historical contours remain vague, the full details indistinct. Does it matter?

What would the name of Titus mean to us without the publicity Racine gave to his love affair with Berenice? Who would know Vespasian without the *vespasiennes* of Paris?

Thousands of diverse waterfowl are drawn to the rich fishing grounds of the Kinnereth, while camping vacationers find relaxation in amateur fishing as well.

Gan Hashlosha at the foot of Mount Gilboa with its abundance of natural pools and waterfalls is a recreational park of great attraction to thousands of picknickers during most of the year (left). Part of the magnificent mosaic covering the floor of the 6th century synagogue found in Beit Alpha, a kibbutz in the Beit She'an valley at the foot of Mount Gilboa. The upper of the two panels seen here show the Ark of the Covenant flanked by traditional Jewish symbols: *menorahs* (seven-branched candelabra), lions, palm trees, *shofar* (ram's horn) etc., while the lower panel represents the Zodiac circle with images of the Seasons in the corners.

The poor emperor who built the Colosseum to perpetuate his fame. The Colosseum was so named only because of the proximity of a colossal statue of Nero. Once the statue had disappeared Nero has come down through the ages to us as a firebug, although he probably did not set fire to Rome! Should this soft-focus effect in which our memory bathes be criticized?

The case of Salome is typical. She danced, removing her seven veils one by one to obtain from King Herod the head of John the Baptist. It was brought to her on a platter. Thanks to the operas by Massenet and Strauss, thanks to the great quantity of paintings, of books and movies, these personages have acquired a face, a body, and even a psychology. Salome: a trollop; Herodias: a bawd; Herod: an old lecher. The latter is especially repugnant. A notorious collaborator, he was placed on the throne of Israel by the Roman occupying powers. He had already been held up to public obloquy by ordering the Slaughter of the Innocents. Newborn babies butchered, that is not easily forgotten. If need be, Fra Angelico, Mazzo-

The valley of Beit She'an (below), south of the Lake of Galilee, is intensively cultivated, abounding in rich and most varied agricultural produce. The Roman amphitheater in Beit She'an (right), testifies to the importance of the town in ancient times, which was one of the Decapolis—the ten independent cities in the Graeco-Roman period.

The Haifa University complex (right) on a narrow ridge of the Carmel commands an incomparable view of scenic beauty. At the foot of the ridge eastward stretches the plain of Zebulun where the country's heaviest industry is located, as well as the oil refineries and Haifa's auxiliary and shipyard harbor at the mouth of the Kishon river. To the west, beneath the wooded slopes of the Carmel sparkles the Mediterranean sea. Below, scientist at work.

This anchor placed over the Haifa-Tel-Aviv highway symbolizes the drama of the illegal immigration of the survivors of the Holocaust, who by means of old and unseaworthy vessels ran the blockade of the British Empire.

A magnificent panoramic view from Mount Carmel of the
Haifa Bay, its harbor and city. On the slopes of the Carmel,
the gold plated dome of the Bahai Shrine dominates the view
of the city as one of its most outstanding landmarks.

lino and Tintoretto are there to refresh our memory.

Reality is different. We have become confused. There were three Herods. The first, called the Great, ordered the Slaughter of the Innocents. The one who allowed himself to be seduced by Salome is Herod-Antipas, and the last, who died at the age of 100 in Rome, was named Herod-Agrippa. But once this confusion is straightened out what does it really change? What counts is that we have retained the dramatic moment: the scene and its meaning. Now, this treasure-store of anecdotes which enriches our hours of meditation is given to us by the Bible.

And Israel is the setting for the Bible.

Look at these ruins: this is where Salome danced. Lean over this hole which time has opened in the stonework: in those caves John the Baptist was imprisoned. His thundering voice could be heard above.

Do you remember Joshua stopping the sun to have time enough to crush the Amorites? That occurred in the Valley of Ayalon between Ramle and Jerusalem.

And tiny David attacking Goliath with his ridiculous sling shot? That meeting took place in these plains on the Beersheba road. While showing you a break in a nearby peak, the guide may add, "In falling, the giant's head split open the rock." If you smile, do so discreetly, for this is the naive poetry which stimulated your memory.

Here is the Ashkelon beach where Samson first met Delilah, who was later to cut his hair and cause his downfall. On this same shore a whale returned Jonah to the light of day.

The *kibbutzim* have covered the Yezreel plain with crops. But beneath the wheat and fruit the land still bears the scars of the past. In Gidona flows a stream and on its banks a thousand years before Jesus Christ, Gideon assembled his warriors to choose three hundred who were "capable of lapping up water without bending their knees." The shadow of Mount Tabor sweeps daily across the Gilboa mountain range where Saul atoned for his sins. On the eve of battle he lamented, for hadn't he again obliged David to flee? Conscience-stricken he implored heaven.

36

Of Turkish construction, Acre's walls and battlements (left) withstood Napoleon's efforts to capture the town. The shallow calm waters of the Bay of Acre and wide beaches of soft sand draw thousands of bathers during the summer season.

Caesarea, the magnificent harbor city founded by Herod the Great in 22 B.C., named by him after Caesar Augustus, his friend and benefactor. The aqueduct (below) and the amphitheater (right) are some of the vestiges of that great ancient city. The amphitheater still serves as an open-air theater for artistic performances and other cultural venues.

The only golf club in Israel situated in present-day Caesarea —a quarter of elegant summer houses and villas and a five-star hotel—draws golf enthusiasts from all over the country.

Yahveh paid no heed. Desperate, breaking the law which forbade consulting "clairvoyants," he went incognito to En-dor. There lived a woman who "possessed a spirit." She recognized the sovereign and raised Samuel's spirit, which said, "Jehovah has departed from you . . . and Jehovah has rent the kingdom out of your hand. . . . Moreover Jehovah will also deliver Israel with you into the hand of the Philistines." Poignant moment: the king, knowing himself lost, fell to the ground, paralysed by fear and horror. The next day he went heavy-hearted to his death. His terrified soldiers fled. Saul was "struck." He urged his armor bearer to kill him. When the latter refused, Saul took his sword and fell upon it.

David soon learned of the ignominious end of the man to whom he owed so much good and so much pain. Wild with grief, he cursed the mountains of Gilboa, saying, "Let there be no dew nor rain upon you, neither fields of offerings." He beseeched his companions: "Publish it not in the streets of Ashkelon; lest the daughters of the Philistines rejoice!" He cried, "How are the

The seashore of Netanya, one of Israel's main summer resorts on the Mediterranean, is teeming with bathers seeking relief from the heat of summer months.

The development of scientifically-based intensive cultivation of the soil has put Israel on the world map of high agricultural expertise, bringing outstanding success in diverse fields, whether in industrial produce such as cotton (left) or rich crops of vegetables (below).

Crop spraying from the air is a commonly used method to ensure high yields of top quality agricultural crops.

The Wingate Institute, the main sports training center, whose graduates serve as physical training instructors in Israeli schools, colleges and armed forces. Some of the institute's outstanding students earned world renown in international competitions.

mighty fallen in the midst of the battle?" He would be king, he knew, but he could not rejoice because of his grief. Perhaps he had a presentiment of his own death, marred by sin.

In Beth-shan one can see today, admirably restored, the ancient Roman theatre. Before it was built, an ancient pagan temple stood there, dedicated to the goddess Astarte. Against its wall the Philistines nailed the naked, decapitated body of King Saul. When the inhabitants of Jabesh heard of this they marched all night to recover his remains. Full of pity and piety they burned and buried the body and then "fasted seven days."

Where the kibbutz of Yezreel now flourishes there was once a vineyard belonging to a certain Naboth. The ruler at that time was Ahab who had married Jezebel. Ill-advised by his wife, he coveted Naboth's vineyard, and to acquire it had him condemned to death. The prophet Elijah was indignant: "Have you killed, and also taken possession?" (I Kings 21:19)

The authors of these tales did not embellish, did not spare the mighty. Nor does

The youth village is a gateway to successful integration of immigrant children into the mainstream of Israeli life. High level secondary education, vocational training and instruction in arts and crafts are provided, as well as recreational and sports activities. The youngsters are encouraged to assume responsibility in taking part in the administration of the villages and planning of cultural events. They develop in the process a sense of dependability, efficiency and independence.

The native produce of Israel: children born in the country are nicknamed *sabra*, after the prickly-pear, fruit of the thorny cactus, since like the native sabra-fruit, they are supposed to be sweet and tender under their bristling exterior. But the citrus tree yields smooth, sweet, golden fruit out of its fragrant blossoms.

Yahveh pardon the sin committed. The greatest personalities in the Bible have the weaknesses of all men. Samson allowed himself to be duped like a child. David, prey to middle-age lust, sent Bathsheba's husband to his death. The pitiless chronicler had mercy on no one. The only one who comes out undamaged is Solomon. Pure and without blemish, the memory of his greatness, of his spirit of justice, of his touching love for the Queen of Sheba, has been kept alive for over three thousand years. Deeply religious, he had precious wood brought from Lebanon to decorate the temple of Jerusalem. King Hiram was happy to send it to him, for Solomon, a man of peace, was on friendly terms with neighboring sovereigns. An astute statesman, he industrialized his country. In Timna in the south, behind enormous rust columns which are still called "Solomon's pillars," a throng of workers extracted and treated copper in "King Solomon's mines." The metal was exported then, as today, by the port of Elath on the Red Sea. It was from there also that his unfortunate fleet set out and was destroyed in a storm. A man of war,

The kibbutz, a collective community whose income based upon agricultural as well as industrial produce, is a unique lifestyle framework of Israeli invention. Left, well-furnished dining hall where wholesome, skillfully prepared food is served to all members—an arrangement that would delight many a beleaguered working-cum-housewife woman. The kibbutz is considered a children's paradise, providing their educational and recreational needs in scope and quality on a level no other system can match.

he levied a special tax to strengthen the fortifications of his capital as well as the two fortresses commanding the eastern and northern roads: Megiddo and Hazor. He had sensed the importance that strategy could have for the cavalry in battle: in Hazor and Megiddo one marvels at the stables and chariot ramps he built.

The grateful population even attributed the existence of the thermal baths of Tiberias to his power. Legend has it that the great king also had supreme control over Hell. For his relaxation he ordered demons to "heat water for his bath." And the cloven hoofs at once got busy in the center of the earth, just under the Sea of Galilee, the pleasant Lake of Gennesaret. Solomon found the water so good that he did not want to deprive future generations of such enjoyment. He knew he was destined to die some day and that the demons would hear of his death and stop working, so he made them deaf. In this way for the last three thousand years those poor devils still have not heard that the king is dead and conscientiously continue to heat water for his bath. High Jewish dignitaries

Kibbutz kitchens (left) are models of modern planning and mechanization, with special emphasis on convenience and efficiency, providing the ladies on duty with as much comfort as can possibly be enjoyed at the proximity of cauldrons. The festival celebrating the beginning of spring harvest in the kibbutz (right) is enjoyed by all, not least by the Japanese volunteer leading the colorful procession.

as well as Greek, Roman, Byzantine, Arab, Turkish, English, and crowds of sufferers from rheumatism have since flocked to Tiberias to bathe in the spring and find a remedy for their ills. Squatting over the emanations of sulfurous steam, or straddling the stone lion now worn out by so many rumps, Bedouin women have tried, are still trying, to cure the worst of all afflictions: sterility.

Of the three great kings, Saul, David, and Solomon, we tend to prefer the second. Is this out of a spirit of democracy? As Regnard said, "Destiny finds pleasure in occasionally allying by a secret bond the scepter and the shepherd's crook." The young shepherd whom God guided to the throne impresses us. As a musician he brightened the black moods of his protector, Saul, by playing the harp. As king he danced before the Ark on the road to Jerusalem. As victim he had to flee the fits of jealousy which endangered his friendship with Saul, who sent soldiers after him to kill him.

He was still very young when, on the banks of the Dead Sea, David took refuge in a cave at En-Gedi. Soldiers with Saul leading

Secular in aspect, yet based upon a deep faith in the guiding hand of Providence, are the holidays of Purim and Hanukka. The gay, dressing-up and marry-making Purim commemorates the foiling of wicked Haman's evil plot against the Jews in ancient Persia. Youngsters dressed up as King Ahasuerus, his queen Esther, their attendants, the wise Mordecai and the wicked Haman have re-enacted the story of Esther year after year, until dressing up and carnival procession (left) became an unseparable feature of the Purim holiday. Hanukka, commemorates the miracle that occurred during the rededication of the Temple in 164 B.C. by the victorious Maccabees. When the *menora* (seven-branched candelabrum) was to be relit, only a small jar of oil could be found. Then the impossible happened: the small quantity of oil kept burning in the great menora for eight days! In memory of this miracle, Jews have celebrated this highlight in their history with an eight-day festival, lighting the Hanukka lights. Below, children lighting Hanukka candles in a kindergarten.

them pursued him. ". . . there was a cave; and Saul went in to cover his feet. And the men of David said unto him, Behold, the day of which Jehovah said unto thee, Behold, I will deliver thine enemy into thy hand and thou shalt do to him as it shall seem good unto thee." But David refused. Quietly in the dark he approached his former protector "and cut off the skirt of Saul's robe privily." Afterwards David followed Saul out of the cave and threw himself at his feet saying, "My lord, the king . . . Jehovah had delivered thee today into my hand . . . and I said I will not put forth my hand against my lord; for he is Jehova's anointed."

A kibbutz has been established on the site, and the water of En-Gedi, "the spring of the kid," still flows from rock to rock, making an oasis out of this corner of the most arid desert on the face of the earth. For here, we are some 13,000 feet below sea level.

Farther south, facing the ancient ford of Cape Molyneux, in a nightmarish landscape, stands the formidable citadel of Massada. The Numantia of the Near East, the Gilbraltar of the Dead Sea, compact, titanic, hol-

Bonfires are lit by children throughout the country on the eve of Lag Ba'omer (33 days of the counting of the sheaths), introducing the beginning of the harvest. According to tradition, it is the presumed date of the death of rabbi Shimon Bar Yohai, the reputed father of the *Cabbala*, in whose honor the bonfires are lit.

The Independence Day celebrations, commemorate the declaration of the re-establishment of the State of Israel on the 15th May 1948, marking the end of the nineteen centuries' long exile. One of the features of the celebration, the lively "depka", a traditional Arab dance executed by an ensemble of the minorities draws hundreds of enthusiastic spectators.

Angry demonstrators in the streets of the capital proclaiming their dissatisfaction with the government do not as a rule add to the décor, but are nevertheless a healthy expression of democracy in the young state.

58

lowed out by a hundred galleries, this huge block was impregnable. Without it the fantastic scenery all around it would very likely not have attained its grandiose appearance of tragedy.

The cataclysm which swallowed up Sodom and Gomorrah also punished man's accomplice, Nature. The hand of God twisted the salt, the stone and the sand to create these mute personages, these gloomy forms, this petrified and silent forest, witnesses of His wrath. Weird, inhuman landscape. Scintillating needles, chimneys from which the wind extracts atonal screams, peaks, mesas, hollows, decaying carcasses of dead wood on the beaches, white and brittle, branches twisted and outstretched like arms imploring a pardon that will never be accorded; sparkling pebbles; impalpable mist of evaporating brooklets where the eye wavers, uncertain; geological strata of a hundred hues, the mountainsides stripped by earthquakes like the nerves of a dissected corpse. Finally, dominating the landscape, proudly erect, the rock of Massada.

Massada comes from Metzuda: fortress.

From the beginning, man recognized its military virtues. This is why it was called Massada. Fortress.

Led by the Hasmonean family the Jews uprose in the second century B.C. against the Greek pretension of introducing pagan idols into the Temple. The sons of the family so badly battered the occupying power that the people nicknamed them the Maccabees: the hammers. One of them, Jonathan, set up a garrison in Massada in order to control the Dead Sea ford and to ward off an eventual attack from the east. This is the first Jewish revolt and a victorious one. Having defeated the Greeks and their satellites in 167 B.C., the Maccabees set up the Hasmonean kingdom, full of glory, which lasted less than a century. The next invader was the most formidable of all. Rome.

The king whom they installed on the throne of Israel, Herod, had difficulties with the Parthians in the east; with Cleopatra, queen of Egypt, in the south. He reinforced Massada, had a palace built and provisions brought. There was a possibility that he might have to take refuge in the impregnable citadel to

Greeted by girl-soldiers upon arrival, new immigrants disembark at the Haifa port. They are assisted throughout the wearying arrival procedures by these charming girls, until their departure for absorption centers, where a six months' sojourn prepares them for better integration in the old-new country.

The *ulpan*, where new immigrants battle with the first and most important obstacle to successful integration—the mastery of Hebrew. For many a beginner Hebrew is ever so much double-Dutch, which nevertheless turns into an articulate command of the language at the term of a six month intensive drill.

Diverse faces of Israel: two young immigrants (left) perusing through the "primer"—the "Gateway to Hebrew", the mastery of which is by no means an easy achievement to accomplish. Right, clockwise: an elderly Yemenite Jew at prayer; a new immigrant from Russian Georgia displaying his chest covered with medals which he earned for valor in World War II; an elderly Moroccan Jew.

withstand a siege while awaiting fresh supplies of Roman legions.

However, it was not until thirty years after the crucifixion of Christ that the second, the Great Revolt of the Jews gave Massada a soul. After the fall of Jerusalem and the destruction of the Temple, while the repressions were being mercilessly carried out, a thousand resistants, most of them belonging to the sect of Zealots, threw themselves into the battle. A battle in the name of honor which lasted three years. We know the details thanks to the description written by the first historian of our era, an unknown officer by the name of Joseph Ben Mattatia. Made prisoner and afterwards attaché to Emperor Vespasian—a Flavian—he assumed, to honor his majestic protector, the pseudonym of Josephus Flavius and wrote a monumental work in memory of his companions in arms: *The Wars of the Jews*.

It was he who interviewed one of the survivors of Massada: one of the two women and five children who had hidden in a cistern at the last moment.

The Roman general Silva had methodically

encircled the site. His legions camped at the foot of the rock. The lay-out of the camps is still clearly visible. That was in the year 70. The defenders stood fast, day after day, until 73, under the command of an inflexible leader: Eleazar Ben Yair. Finally Silva succeeded in erecting an extraordinary work of art; a steep ramp which climbed up to storm the upper plateau. His men reached the outside wall and set fire to it. Night fell.

The Zealots held council. Victory had slipped away from them. Had they ever really believed in it? A collective suicide was decided upon. At least they would die free.

Having kissed their wives and children the men stretched out on the floor, arms enlaced. Ten men, picked at random, went from one to the other stabbing and cutting the throats offered to them. The horrible carnage went on for hours. At dawn when it was completed the ten soldiers again drew lots to determine which of them was to put his nine companions to death. The remaining man made a final check on the corpses to be sure that none still had need of his services, set fire to the fortress and killed himself. In the

Sunset over the Mediterranean bathing the horizon in all the glory of the spectrum.

morning the legionaries, who had seen many other gory scenes in their time, were "struck dumb by the spectacle awaiting them".

Enslaved, the Jewish nation experienced a third and last uprising in 132 A.D. The Emperor Hadrian decided to have done with Jewish particularism. In this connection it should be made clear that the monotheism in a pagan world was easily confused at that time with the intensive propagation of Christ's teachings. Judaism and Christianity did not become separate until much later. Until then the "bearers of the good word" naturally received hospitality in Jewish communities. They preached in the synagogues. Now, their teachings contradicted the multiple faith, the philosophy of conquest, the morality of the strong, which guided Roman life. Hadrian forbade these meetings, which showed too modern a trend for his liking and, above all, circumcision, by which the Jews distinguished themselves from the Gentiles.

An indignant Bar Kochba called his brothers to arms and the people followed him. The wise and scholarly old Rabbi Akiba—

Lined with outdoor cpfes and fashionable shops, the spacious Kings of Israel Square in Tel-Aviv is a favorite promenade of mums and tots in the morning hours, while in the evenings; the lovely illu'ination and colored fountains attract Tel-Avivians from all over the city for a leisurely stroll. Occasionally open-air concerts of light classical music are held there on summer evenings, always well attended by thousands of enthusiastic listeners. In the background the Municipality building.

The reconstructed quarter of old Jaffa. Since the most ancient times Jaffa has been an important seaport on the eastern Mediterranean. In the past fifteen years the narrow twisting alleys of the old town, descending from the hill to the harbor, were reconstructed and turned into a charming and pictur-esque quarter, where many artists chose to set up their homes as well as their art galleries. A lovely park was laid out on the slope over the ruins of the ancient town, from which unfolds a magnificent view of Tel-Aviv and the sea.

The skyline of Tel-Aviv, view from the mound of ancient Jaffa. In 1909 a group of Jewish inhabitants of Jaffa built over the desolate sand dunes north of the town a modern suburb which they called *Tel-Aviv*, the "Hill of Spring". In 1921 Tel-Aviv was granted municipal rights, and from that moment on the town began to develop at an ever-increasing pace, to become the largest and most modern city of Israel. Greater Tel-Aviv now counts nearly half a million inhabitants. Bustling with activity, vigorous and dynamic, the city is the center of light industry as well as of tourism, its seashore lined with luxury hotels that cater to thousands of tourists. Two excellent universities, numerous musea, theaters and concert halls complete the picture of this tremendously alive, stimulating metropolis.

"Thou shalt love thy neighbor as thyself" — himself buckled on his sword. Seeing this wildly aroused fanaticism, Rome vacillated and retreated right to the walls of Jerusalem. But the holy city did not fall into the hands of the insurrectionists. The uprising had broken out in the name of the Eternal Father and He had refused His soldiers access to His city.

With this adverse blow the warriors saw the sign of a divine punishment. The defeat discouraged them.

The one-hundred-year-old Rabbi Akiva was skinned alive in Caesarea. Bar Kochba succumbed in Bethar in 135. Exasperated, the Romans gave no quarter. Jerusalem had no longer existed as such since 70. It was called *Aelia Capitolina*. It was henceforth forbidden to Jews under penalty of death. Reduced to slavery, ejected, exiled, the survivors scattered throughout the empire. This dispersion was called the *diaspora*.

That was the end, an end that, in misfortune, the elected race doggedly continued to hope only temporary. During two thousand years, believer or non-believer, wherever he

was, the Jew would say, "If I forget you, O Jerusalem, may my right hand wither."

For almost twenty years, until 1967 to pass from the Old Testament to the New, to tread on the soil of His Passion, to climb His Calvary, Christ would have to present himself at the Mandelbaum gate of Jerusalem in the center of the city. The Jordanian guards would not let him enter because he was a Jew.

From the Hill of Bad Counsel the visitor may contemplate the Mount of Olives and the Garden of Gethsemane. He goes to Ramath Rahel to see, in the distance, Bethlehem and the Church of the Nativity. In the ravine where a tree was felled to construct the instrument of torture, the Valley of the Cross, stands an ancient Orthodox monastery. On one of the slopes of the ravine stands the ancient city, recently constructed; on the other, the administrative city, the *Kiryah*, with the parliament: *Knesset*, the official buildings, the ministries, the university, the museums.

In the pleasant village of Ein Karem—"source of the vineyard"—at the foot of the

Hadassah, the best equipped hospital in the Middle East, are the catholic Church of the Visitation as well as another, an Orthodox one. They were built in memory of the touching meeting of two expectant mothers who were related. Already stirring within them were John the Baptist and Jesus.

On Mount Zion, is the "Upper Room," scene of the Last Supper, where He met with the "Twelve" and established the Eucharist. It was also in this room that He appeared before the apostles after his crucifixion. "Jesus came and stood in the midst and saith unto them, Peace be unto you." And He said further "that repentance and remission of sins should be preached in his name unto all the nations, beginning from Jerusalem." The tomb of King David, from whom Jesus descended, is also on Mount Zion, even if that glorious ancestor is really buried on the Ophel with the other kings of Judah.

Finally, here too stands the Church of the Dormition where Mary closed her eyes. As soon as she had entered her last sleep, Jesus called His Mother using the words of the Song of Songs: "Rise up, my love, my fair

70

The Helena Rubinstein Pavilion of modern art, part of the Tel-Aviv Museum. Exhibitions held at the Pavilion are always assured of a vast attendance due to its high artistic standards and the Tel-Avivians' affection for plastic arts.

one, and come away." And so she ascended into heaven body and soul.

In Galilee no frontier hampers the Christian pilgrim. Christ probably went on foot with His Mother to Cana which is a stone's throw from Nazareth. They were invited to a wedding. Mary, seeing that the wine was gone, urged Her Son to do something about it. He refused at first, saying, "Woman, what have I to do with thee? mine hour is not yet come." But Mary, with the gentle obstinacy of a mother, turned confidently to the servants: "Whatsoever he saith unto you, do it." Jesus complied, changing the water into wine. Cana, Tabgha where He multiplied bread and fish to feed the multitude, Naim, where on His command, a dead man returned to life, Tabor where He went for His transfiguration in the company of three disciples, and Daburriya—Deborah—where the other nine awaited them—all those holy places still exist today because of their past history. They are now but poor villages, rich only in the fervor of memory.

He did not like the city of Tiberias, full of Herod's soldiers, whom He despised and considered a "fox." But He was happy to meditate on the banks of the lake where His fishermen friends worked. He walked along its edge and occasionally even walked on the waters and calmed the waves. He returned there: "This was now the third time that Jesus was revealed to the disciples, after that he was raised from the dead." And He said to Simon whom He called Peter, "Feed my sheep." It was in Migdal, nowadays but some ruins of a tower, where He met Mary Magdalene.

On the Mount of Beatitudes where the view stretches out far beyond the Lake of Tiberias, the Sermon on the Mount was preached: "Blessed are . . ." But before this, after spending the night in prayer, "He called his disciples; and He chose from them twelve whom He named apostles: Simon, whom He named Peter—("And on this Rock I shall build my Church")—and Andrew his brother, and James and John, and Philip, and Bartholomew, and Mathew, and Thomas, and James the son of Alphaeus, and Simon who was called the Zealot, and Judas the son of James, and Judas Iscariot, who became a traitor."

Nazareth, this town of renown, is half Christian and half Moslem. Fief of the Franciscans who have for seven centuries guarded the Holy Places, it welcomes hundred of thousands of tourists as well as pilgrims each year. The new basilica of the Annunciation now stands on the very site of the church which the Crusaders had built over the ancient altar which bears the words of John the Evangelist: "And the Word became flesh."

Mary lived in Nazareth during the time She was engaged to Joseph the carpenter. She returned there later with Her family. Here the Child spent His adolescence. The fountain where She drew water still bears Her name. And a church was built on the spot where She learned that the crowd wanted to kill Jesus. He had gone to the synagogue and read from the book of the prophet Isaiah: "The Spirit of the Lord is upon me; because he anointed me to preach good tidings to the poor: He hath sent me to proclaim release to the captives and recovering of sight to the blind, to set at liberty them that are bruised, to proclaim the acceptable year of the Lord." Then, closing the

book, he added, "Today hath this scripture been fulfilled in your ears." Praised by some, mocked by others, urged by all to prove His words by performing a miracle, He replied: "No prophet is acceptable in his own country." Filled with wrath they cast Him out of the city and led Him to the brow of a hill in order to push Him headlong. Did this scene of violence really take place at *Djebel-el-Qafse* as visitors are told? In any case, the crowd had to await Easter for the sacrifice. For that day in Nazareth it is said that "... He passing through the midst of them went His way." He went down to Capernaum where he exorcized a demented man and healed the afflicted.

The Jewish guides do not enter the basilica of the Annunciation with their clients. Not for religious reasons. The Christian Arabs are assured, by their *unions*, the monopoly of the visit. Israel is full of such contradictions. The respect for the liberty of others, the sense of democracy are developed to such a degree that it is probably the only country in the world where, were He to return, Jesus would be allowed to preach for three years

74

The flag decorated entrance to the Koffler accelerator on inauguration day, at the Weizman Institute of Science in Rehovot. Established in 1944 by friends of Haim Weizman, the eminent scientist who four years later was called to become Israel's first President, the Institute has attracted the finest scientific brains from all over the world. Its departments for applied mathematics, biophysics, organic chemmistry, physics, isotope and polymer research, electronics, microbiology, genetics and optics are among the most advanced in the world.

as before, even if His actions annoyed the government.

For the first Christians the fish was a sign of their faith. The letters forming the word, in Greek, correspond to the initials of Jesus-Christ-son-of-God-the-Savior. A thousand years after them their descendants erected crosses symbolizing their faith—and also, alas, the tombs in the cemeteries. One cannot talk about Jews without saying a word about anti-Semitism; one cannot speak of Israel without mentioning the Crusades. The two phenomena are related: the exile lasted two thousand years, the persecution a thousand.

During the Roman Empire the Jew was neither more nor less suspect than any other ethnic or religious minority. But the others, the pagans, proceeded to exchange gods, to adopt others. Not the Jews. They had only one and guarded Him jealously. Along came the first Christians. They provoked, they preached. Now, they were usually of Jewish origin. Judaism is exclusive. One is Jewish only by one's mother: the incontestable filiation, the proof by nine months of a relationship desired by the Eternal Father. Quite

to the contrary, the Christian evangelizes and recruits. Nevertheless, it was difficult at first to distinguish between the Jew-who-does-not-believe-Jesus-was-the-Messiah and the Jew-who-believes-Jesus-was-the-Messiah. Both went to the synagogue and worshipped one God. Proselytism clashed with the spirit of authority, however tolerant it was. Spiritual preaching bordered on political propaganda. This had already occurred in Palestine and had ended in bloody riots.

The situation changed in the fourth century. During a very difficult battle a cross appeared before the Emperor Constantine who cried out, *"In hoc signo vinces"*: under the sign of the cross you will vanquish. Victorious, he was converted. Having become official, the Church treated the Jews as a negligible detail; it was too busy establishing itself. In moving his capital, Constantine took a cross to Byzantium and left one in Rome. The shadow cast by the latter required a century and a half to reach France, but it finally crossed the Alps. In turn, Clovis, who had married a Christian, exclaimed on the field of battle, "God of Clothilda," etc.

The establishment of one of the first agricultural settlements in the late 19th century by the young pioneers who left the confines of their eastern European ghettos, Rishon-le-Zion (the first in Zion, in Hebrew), meant not only a return to the Promised Land, but was symbolic of the return to the *land*— the vine, corn and fruit. Today, Rishon-le-Zion is famous for its vast wine-cellars, where high-quality vintage wines and liqueurs mature slowly in the huge vats.

Bishop Remi did the rest. Christianity took five hundred years to cover Europe. It was only in the dawn of the year 1000 that Charlemagne was to convert the Saxons *en masse*.

Meanwhile, in the seventh century the Revelation came to Mohammed. For the Mohammedan, to impose by the sword his religious convictions became a sacred duty. Islam began to storm the Mediterranean shores and, having gone all around them, invaded the European continent. The true conflict, under the guise of spiritual opposition, was between the East and the West. Going beyond ideology it became political. The Jew found himself caught in the crossfire. Earlier his monotheistic reasoning represented an incontestable progress over the primitive philosophical structure of the pagans. Henceforth, he was faced with two mass movements whose arguments were on the same order as his own ideologically, but which, on the matter of conversion, knew no bounds. Neither the Cross nor the Crescent balked at knife-at-the-throat conversions. The Christian proselytism was a system of

diffusing a faith which saves souls. Mohammedan belief was simpler: whoever does not worship Allah is not fit to live. Nonetheless, Islam showed itself to be more tolerant as soon as it had conquered an empire.

The Jew was no longer a negligible detail, because of the economic, cultural and administrative role he had come to play. Under those three aspects he represented a bridge between East and West, since due to the dispersion he had relatives, friends, coreligionists, in short, contacts, throughout the world. He was an integral part of intellectual and scientific circles; he carried out international commerce through his relationships; he invented the bank and the check; he was often a member of the government. It was important to win him over to one's side.

Islam resorted only sporadically to coercion. This depended on the reigning prince, for the attitude of the authorities was governed by his personal temperament. But, quite to the contrary, from one pope to the next the Church maintained a consistent policy.

Of the Cross and the Crescent, it was the

The nuclear reactor (below) at Nahal Sorek near Rishon-le-Zion, where nuclear energy is used for scientific research. Apprentices in the aircraft industries (right) mastering the complex workmanship of this highly specialized profession.

The youngsters' technical training combined with theoretical studies will turn them into superbly skilled professionals in one of the most important fields of modern life.

The ever-burning furnaces of the Vulcan steel foundries supply most of the steel used in aircraft, armaments and fine machinery industries.

Cross that spilled more blood. This was due to the fact that Islam had no tests of strength between the spiritual and temporal powers. The caliph was also Commander of the Believers. If he was bloodthirsty there were killings. If he was good-natured one lived and let live. Now, the first mission of the Vicar of Christ was to impose his authority on the princes, who in turn tried to impose theirs on him. The moral supremacy of the papacy, endlessly questioned, required political power to grow stronger. The latter could be acquired only by the unity of thought. In a similar effort to enlarge their states and to unify them, the kings tried to weaken the Church's authority, even to subjugate it. But the Church and the Throne allied themselves against their common enemy, the barbaric invader. The Crusades were a distraction from their interminable quarrel, and Islam a permanent danger to them both. From this situation anti-Semitism was accidentally born.

The Middle Ages can never be understood without giving the proper importance to religious belief. A wholehearted, complete, unconditional, boundless faith. God was everyone's preoccupation. Whether it was a question of ignorance, of superstition—alchemy, magic, witchcraft—or of culture and progress—the universities and schools were in the hands of the priests—the least movement of the mind or body involved God, was controlled, even dictated by Him. The common man was subdued, the knight, the lord, the king was elevated only by the will of the Omnipotent. There were, of course, the disbelievers, the impious, the blasphemers, but the existence of God: the Blessed Trinity, Allah, or Yahveh, was questioned nowhere.

Nor was there any question of atheism. That too would come from the Jews, the selfsame people who had already introduced the concept of one God. Henri Estienne, in 1566, sensed the trend and affirmed in *Apology for Herodotus*: "One sees people who have not yet become atheists but who are looking for the way leading there." And E. Moland, now long forgotten, wrote in *Systems* (1772) à propos of Spinoza:

The biggest textile industries in Israel, "Ata", employing thousands of workers, constitute an entire township. The plant enjoys a high reputation of quality and efficiency, its products carrying, on both, local and foreign markets, the mark of fine workmanship and finishing. Seen here is the highly sophisticated electronic production control system at the Ata plant.

"Then a small, long-nosed Jew with a pasty complexion,
Poor but satisfied, pensive and withdrawn,
A subtle and trite mind, less read than known,
Hiding under the mantle of Descartes, his master,
Tiptoed up to the Divine Being:
Excuse me, he said, almost in a whisper,
But just between you and me, I don't believe you exist."

But this was several centuries later: we are still on the eve of the Crusades. With the proper perspective we can discover a political and national inspiration behind the great actions which shook the Dark Ages. It emanated imperceptibly from the avidity of governments. The lord who wanted to enlarge his domain, the king who subjugated his vassals for the purpose of increasing his own power, could very well have been working toward essentially selfish goals. They nonetheless followed an evolution in the State's philosophies of which, more often than not, they were scarcely conscious. Out of the desire for unification, dawning nationalism was not necessarily recognizable. Economic

Bird's-eye view of the Old City of Jerusalem. Top right, dominating the view, is the platform of the Temple Mount, where the Dome of the Rock mosque stands on the site of the ancient Temple of the Jews.

expansion was perhaps, for all that, required for the development of exchanges. Feudalism was a stage on the road to capitalism.

At first, the East-West conflict did not appear as such. It is true that man's lowest instincts hide under the most irreproachable cloak: the more sinister the plot hatched in the house, the higher the facade. Hypocrisy, said La Rochefoucauld, is the homage that vice pays to virtue. However, the Middle Ages were not yet hypocritical. To claim that our ancestors, at the moment they were going into the battle which is still going on, were uniformly cynical would be to commit a monumental error. They sincerely believed in trial by ordeal. They were convinced that the hand of an innocent plunged into boiling water would come out unhurt, while that of the guilty would be burned. They were certain that God would protect them in battle because they were fighting His cause. Psychological lucidity, from Charlemagne to Charles V, would have made the Renaissance impossible.

It was with a pure heart, and noble enthusiasm that the man of the Middle Ages set

86

Ever since the destruction of the Second Temple in 70 C.E., its only vestige, the Western Wall, became the holiest site of Judaism, and has drawn through the ages, as it still does today, countless multitudes of Jews, who came to lament over the ruin of their Temple, thus earning the site its name in all languages but Hebrew—the "Wailing Wall". The part of the wall visible today is but a third of its original height—the remainder lies buried under rubble accumulated during centuries, over which the modern pavement was laid. Since the Six Day War, free access to the Wall has been assured to all, and the narrow alley which had enclosed it had to be enlarged into a piazza, to contain the endless stream of visitors and worshippers, especially on the three pilgrimage holidays, Succoth, Passover and Shavuoth (right). On the Temple Mount esplanade, the Dome of the Rock mosque (upper left), its golden dome towering over the octagonal structure, is a marvel of Islamic architecture—covered with resplendent mosaics of geometric design, and magnificent arched stained-glass windows of exquisite beauty.

Muslim worshippers throng on festival days to the el-Aksa mosque (below), the one "most removed" (from Mecca), from which, according to Moslem tradition, the Prophet Mohammed started his voyage to heaven on his favorite mare el-Burak. The mosque, situated on the southern end of the Temple esplanade, the side facing Mecca, is the third holiest site of Islam after Mecca and Medina. Countless pilgrims throughout the ages, carrying the cross, have retraced the footsteps of Jesus on the Via Dolorosa (right), stopping reverently at each of the Fourteen Stations on the way to Calvary.

The most picturesque of the Old City gateways, the northern, commonly known as the Damascus Gate, through which passes the road to Nablus and Damascus. Built over, and following the groundplan of the 3rd century Roman gate underneath it, the gate is still called *Bab el-Amud* ("Gate of the Column") in Arabic, in memory of a pillar that stood behind it in Roman times. Of Mameluke workmanship, this gate with its plethora of ornate battlements is one of the finest monuments of the period (14th–16th centuries).

The teeming bazaars of the Old City offer wares as variegated as human nature may desire and more. Scattered amid the motley display of garments, carpets, trinkets, sheepskin coats and copperware, is a galore of spices and pickles, charcoaled *shashlik-kebab*, its smoke filling the air and mingling with the delicious smell of baking *pitta* (flat Arab bread) buns and elaborate nut-and-honey pastry—an Eden for the aroma-conscious connoisseur. Rubbing shoulders in the bustling narrow lanes, are economy-minded shoppers, heavily laden donkeys, nuns, skullcapped pious Jews, stately black-veiled Arab women balancing incredible weights on their heads, black-clad Greek-Orthodox priests and plain admirers of teeming motley humanity. A riot of garb and headdress and color.

Of Mameluke construction, the medieval, vaulted streets (left) in the Old City of Jerusalem awe and enchant the visitor. One of the pages of glory in the history of Judaism is the development of high quality education of children in family and in the community. Parents were expressly enjoined by the sages: "Teach your children Scripture, so that they have understanding throughout their entire life by continually reading the Law of God." From the age of four, boys from orthodox families are required to study the Torah (the Law). *Heder* (right), the primary school where the boys memorize the sacred texts, while one little dreamer is immersed deeply in thought.

out on a Crusade. It was in the very depths of their beings that serfs, the lords, and kings feared the year One Thousand, with the most absolute conviction that they were under the solemn obligation to deliver the Holy Sepulcher. A mass movement cannot be created without the sincerity of the masses. Here, the leaders themselves were imprisoned at the same intellectual level as the common man of that day. If the Crusades and adventure helped their personal affairs, so much the better! That proved that God intended to reward their virtue. And if it didn't help them? Never mind. They must have sinned and it would be atoned for by departing for the Holy Land. The most authentic faith gave to the war its badge of nobility.

As for the horror and cruelty, this was current and common to both sides. Blood, whether one's own or one's enemy's was shed in the name of the highest ideal: it didn't count. One killed, one was killed, but not without God's noting, not without His consent that such and such a man was to suffer and die.

After the systematic massacre of the Jews,

Panoramic view of the hill by the Valley of the Cross on the summit of which stands the Knesset, Israel's Parliament, completed in 1966. It consists of four storeys, three of which are underground. The square building, with its flat roof supported by columns running along its four sides, produces an effect at once of simplicity and subdued elegance.

during the sacking of Beziers at the time of the Albigensian Crusade, an atrocious order has been attributed to the abbot Arnauld de Citeaux. When the Crusaders asked him how they could spare the good Christians, he is said to have replied, "Kill them all, God will recognize his own." And he firmly believed it. The contrary was not even imaginable. In any case, even if it is false, this spine-chilling anecdote indicates the pulse of the time, gives food for thought.

In that grandiose conflict the Jew found himself crushed under the immensity of the methods employed, under the universality of the blow. He belonged to a militarily un-organizable minority. He made the mistake of belonging to a third religious group sorely lacking in defenders, unarmed, dispersed. Judaism, which was never a mass movement, was no longer up-to-date. It was the creed of a few isolated men, united here and there in communities exposed to blows from both sides. And the blows kept pouring.

Europe prayed and armed itself. However, an army cannot be recruited without doubt-ful elements mixing with the idealistic. There

96

The Knesset at a sitting. The House of Representatives is composed of 120 members elected by the vote of all citizens above the age of eighteen in democratic elections held every four years. The Prime Minister and his Cabinet are directly responsible to the Knesset. The horse-shoe table in the center is occupied by the members of the government, rear desks by members of the different factions and the gallery is reserved for the press and visitors.

On the outskirts of Jerusalem, towering above the pastoral terraced slopes of Ein Karem is the Hadassah-Hebrew University Medical Center. Built in 1961 to replace the original hospital on Mount Scopus to which approach was denied by the Jordanian authorities after 1948, it is today the most modern complex of its kind in the Middle East. It comprises a hospital of over 800 beds, schools of medicine, pharmacology, dentistry and nursing, a Cancer Research and Treatment Institute, and last but not least, an out-patient clinic treating over a thousand patients daily. The Center bears proudly its sponsor's name—*Hadassah,* the outstanding in their devotion Women's Zionist Organization of America.

On one of the spurs of Mount Herzl in Jerusalem, marked from afar by a tall iron pillar, stands Yad Va-Shem, the monument consecrated to the memory of the six million Jews, victims of the most systematic genocide history ever knew. The Hebrew words *yad va-shem*—hand (or monument) and name—are taken from prophet Isaiah's sublime verset: "I will give them in my house and within my walls a monument and . . . an everlasting name which shall not be cut off" (56:5). The Memorial Shrine, a square mass of black basalt boulders supporting a conic roof of reinforced concrete is striking in its austerity. The entrance leads through iron-wrought gates, the work of an outstanding Israeli sculptor, the late David Palombo. Inside, the floor of grey-black mosaic carries twenty-two panels, each bearing a gruesome name of infamy: Dachau, Auschwitz, Majdanek . . . Through a square aperture in the roof, sunlight falls upon

the eternal flame burning above an urn of human ashes brought from the crematoria of the main concentration camps. The Yad Va-Shem compound is approached through the Avenue of Righteous Gentiles, where each tree commemorates or is planted by an individual or a community, who in the face of mortal peril to themselves and their dear ones extended a helping hand to their Jewish fellow-men.

Next to the Shrine is a building comprising the museum, library, reading-room and archives of the Holocaust, containing thousands of heart-rending documents, photographs, diaries and books, as well as names of those who perished. At the entrance to this gruesome museum, the monument (left) commemorates the heroic uprisings of the ghettoes doomed to annihilation.

The Wolfson residential quarter, comprising the high-rise and habitat style architecture, affords its residents one of the finest views in Jerusalem. It is situated on a hill overlooking the scenic beauty of the Valley of the Cross, where the 11th century Greek-Orthodox monastery, resting on Byzantine foundations, stands on the traditional site where grew the tree from which Jesus' Cross was made.

existed in the West poverty-stricken multitudes whose presence endangered the established order. They had nothing to lose and asked for nothing better than to enlist. Eyes bright, palms itching, they listened to the fiery speeches of preachers and shivered with righteous indignation. However, their impatience to receive some of the bliss promised in the Hereafter aroused a desire for immediate revenge in this world. It was the first time they had been accorded any social importance aside from that of servitude. To the cry, "Let us go out to deliver Christ's Tomb!" they replied by a roar, "His assassins are in our midst!"

And so they tried their hand on the Jewish communities. It was a form of practice like any other for troops totally lacking in experience.

History books pass over in delicate silence the slaughter, pillage, murder and rape which followed, and the burning of whole towns. The Infidel was an enemy and, after all, the Jew, too, was an Infidel. The horde of ragamuffins had taken the Cross and had

A superb view of Bethlehem (left) and its surroundings unfolds from the belfry of one of the numerous churches of the town whose name remains engraved in mankind's memory as the home-town of King David and the birthplace of Jesus. Another landmark in Bethlehem, especially revered by orthodox Jewish women, is the presumed Tomb of Rachel (below), Jacob's beloved wife. Here Rachel died in childbirth of her second son, Benjamin, ". . . and was buried on the way to . . . Bethlehem, and Jacob set up a pillar upon her grave" (Genesis 35:19).

One of the most hallowed shrines of Christianity, the Church of Nativity in Bethlehem. From the second century on tradition has placed the site of Jesus' birth in a cave near the village of Bethlehem. Over the revered grotto Constantine the Great had built the first Church of Nativity in 326. It was replaced by Justinian in the 6th century with the Basilica as it stands at present. Thousands of worshippers and pilgrims flock to the church, throughout the year, but

especially so to celebrate the midnight High Mass on Christmas. The church and the square in front of it are packed beyond capacity when the great star over Bethlehem com-memorates Jesus' birth. In the grotto of Nativity (below) the traditionally exact place of Jesus' birth is marked by a silver star dating from the 18th century.

Some four miles southeast of Bethlehem, a volcano-shaped mountain dominates the landscape on the verge of the Judean desert. Here, on top of the high conical hill, Herod the Great built one of his mighty fortresses, Herodium. Of circular shape, with four round towers placed crosswise in the massive wall to guard its approaches, the fortress was virtually impenetrable. Herod had the fortress provided with all the necessary amenities—dwelling rooms for the king and his attendants, a bath, a banqueting hall with walls and floors covered with frescoes and mosaics, a synagogue and an enclosed garden—all marked with the luxury and elegance this Hellenized Jewish king loved to surround himself with. According to Josephus Flavius Herod was buried with great pomp in a magnificent sepulcher in the Herodium fortress, but the tomb has not been discovered so far.

now and henceforth, without even leaving their country, earned a place in Paradise. They were called "The Poor." They would remain such.

They acquired a taste for murder and looting. Their activity began to take on social importance, to menace property in general. They were hastily dispatched to be rid of. Led by Peter the Hermit and Gautier Sans Avoir, without the least military training, these amateurs preceded the Crusades of professionals, the knights. Their appalling adventure left the road to the East strewn with cadavers. They knew only how to kill. And to die. For they dropped like flies, they too, decimated by brawls, illness, skirmishes, the resistance of towns rightfully terrified of their passage. Any Jewish community which had the misfortune to find itself in their path fell victim to the tragically absurd quid pro quo: to be killed in the name of the God of Love. The unfortunate and ill-starred *Crusade of the Poor* never reached the Holy Land. The sultan of Micaea exterminated the last members of that lamentable herd of assassins on the border of Asia.

This practice was to be continued. The following crusades were to follow the same pattern. The ecclesiastical hierarchy could not afford the luxury of looking closely into the distribution of indulgences. Not until the second half of the twentieth century did the Catholic Church officially absolve the Jews of the crime of deicide. On the road of Christ's avengers, German cities now offer hospitality to Jews—as long as they can pay for it. As for Palestine, it goes without saying that the warriors granted no quarter.

For the time being the Jew was only a victim of a certain moral climate. Cruelty prevailed. Life had little value. Superstition took the upper hand over faith. But finally, and for centuries, carnage became a method of governing. The Crusaders seized Constantinople—Christian but Orthodox—sacked it and wreaked more havoc than the Turks ever did. The Albigensian Crusade also set Christians against Christians. Until then Judaism had only had to face anarchic circumstances. Henceforth, anti-Semitism was going to become organized.

Kings and popes in common accord cre-

Originally quarries for a special type of chalk much used by the Byzantines for their vast building activity, the underground caves of Beit Govrin are favorite sites of excursionists of all ages.

Hebron is today renowned for its fine glass industry, consisting usually of small one-family enterprises. In one of the small drab workshops, a glass-blower turns the jewel-colored glass melting in the furnace into lovely vases, jars and bowls. Glass industry, one of the oldest in the Holy Land, began thousands of years ago on its northern coasts. Phoenician glass was famous throughout antiquity and the Middle Ages. The Crusaders brought the secrets of the craft to Europe, from which developed the high art of Venetian glass. Fleeing the Inquisition in the 15th century, many Italian Jews returned to their ancient homeland bringing with them the art of glass-blowing from the world-famous Venetian factories. They settled in Hebron and thus re-established the ancient craft in the Holy Land.

The Tomb of the Patriarchs in Hebron, standing above the Machpelah cave. Hebron's history begins in dim antiquity; it was already a thriving town when Abraham and his retinue arrived there around 1800 B.C. Here dwelt Abraham when his wife Sarah died and he buried her "in the cave of the field of Machpelah east of Hebron" which he had bought from Ephron for "four hundred shekels of silver, according to the weights current among the merchants" (Genesis 23:16–20). Here, he too was laid to rest, then his son Isaac and Rebecca his wife, and later Jacob and Leah. The tradition of the site of this cave goes at least as far back as the period of the Second Temple. King Herod surrounded it with the massive high wall which remained standing intact since then. Its smooth base and pillastered upper part (the crenellated top and minaret were added later) show how the Temple Wall in Jerusalem once looked. The Byzantines covered the Herodian enclosure with a roof, turning it into St. Abraham's church. With the Arab invasion in the 7th century it became the Mosque of Ibrahim, and, but for a short interval during the Crusader rule, it has remained such to this day. Although one of the holiest sites of Jewry, the Machpelah compound was inaccessible to Jews for nearly eight centuries, beyond the seventh step of the entrance stairway. Since the Six Day War, the Tomb of the Patriarchs is open to pilgrims and visitors of all faiths.

ated the Inquisition to repress heresy. It was claimed to be indispensable in maintaining the unity of the Church and the Throne. It would not stop the Reformation. With Torquemada, the Grand Inquisitor of Spain, was born the notion of racism, of *sangre limpia*. To the sin of deicide was added that of tainted blood. Converted by fair means or foul, the *converso* was no longer safe; having adopted the Christian faith, the Jew—and the Moor as well—was still accused of returning to his original faith, was burned, his possessions confiscated, his descendants ostracized.

While this was going on in the Vatican, the kings pursued their own designs: the submission of the great feudal lords, territorial conquests, the unification of their kingdoms. During the expeditions to the Holy Land or to the south of France for the repression of the Catharians, the great and mighty discovered that they could kill two birds with one stone: eliminate undesirables and seize their property, bag and baggage. The Templars never assassinated Christ but they certainly paid for it anyway.

The persecution of the Jews was an extremely profitable practice. The Jews were driven out and their property fattened the royal treasury. The Jews were allowed to return if they could pay the fine. The Jews were tolerated if they paid a special tax.

Their role in society was no longer a monopoly on international relations. The Bank passed into Italian hands. Venice and Francois I flirted dangerously, trafficking with the Turks, and Berbers. The ends of the 13th, 14th, and 15th centuries were marked by "permanent" deportations in France, England and Spain.

The survivors had to survive. Their activity was strictly limited: manual labor, small stores and exchange, that is, the usury of money passing from hand to hand, the diminishing weight of a coin which is *used* up. They will be reproached for practicing these trades to which they were condemned. It will be said that they practiced magic but the entire Middle Ages was dominated by witchcraft, alchemy, and pacts with the Devil. With the arrival of the Reformation, Christians again began to slaughter one another; why would they spare the Jews? The Jews

Wild flowers of Israel, the glory of its countryside in spring. Clockwise, anemones, a wild orchid, a peony, and a wild tulip, are some of the protected species along with daffodils, cyclamen and irises.

were blamed for famine, drought, epidemics. Any anti-Jewish measure taken by the authorities resulted in an increase in government revenue; any slaughter of the Jews, followed by looting, allowed a momentary alleviation of the misery of the humble called to help themselves from others' plates.

Perhaps, on hearing the recital of these horrors, the modern mind would feel regret and point out the purity of intention. Unfortunately butchery pays. Whether the victims were the Albigenses, the Templars or the Jews—the Crusades, the Inquisition, the deportations, exterminations, pogroms, genocides, drew blood that was worth its weight in gold.

It went on for centuries, culminating with Hitlerism.

To ask why they let themselves be massacred without defending themselves is like wondering why ten armed men can get the better of one unarmed prisoner. Their only recourse was prayer. It may not have saved lives but it saved thought. The spirit was transmitted from one victim to the next. To ask why they complied, why they didn't fight back, is to forget the reasons why the Christian martyrs allowed themselves to be thrown to wild beasts without offering resistance. A desire for self-sacrifice does not explain everything. There exists, consciously or unconsciously, a sense of human dignity, of liberty, which sustains the individual. At the dawn of the twentieth century the Jew, nonetheless, emerged from his trials in possession of a detestable reputation. Was it possible even to examine the accusations formulated against him? The Dreyfus Affair shows us the atmosphere of the times. But though anti-Semitism was not about to give up its superstitions, here and there the voice of intelligence succeeded in making itself heard.

Half a century later, public opinion was stirred, for the first time, by the heroic uprising of the Warsaw ghetto. Naturally, humanity had a guilty conscience for having allowed a nation to perpetrate the crime of assassination six million times, for non-assistance to persons in danger. In short, that sharp reaction came just in time. A few years later, in 1948, the Jews, fighting one against

115

Flocks of Beduin sheep and a university are not, so it seems, in each other's way, but rather blend together into a fascinating landscape. This is the Beersheba University, named after David Ben Gurion, the visionary who dreamt and strove to make the Negev desert flourish again. Tradition attributes the founding of Beersheba to Abraham for here he had dug a well and "planted a tamarisk tree in Beersheba, and called there on the name of the Lord" (Genesis 21:31–33). Finds from excavations of the ancient mound indicate that it was already inhabited in Chalcolithic times. On the fringe of the Negev wilderness, Beersheba continued to exist till the Byzantine times, and was abandoned in the Middle Ages. A few streets of low mud-houses and a mosque were put up by the Turks in 1908 to be used by the Beduins as a trading center. In 1948, when Beersheba was taken by the Israeli forces, the dusty, sleepy townlet began developing on a large scale into a modern university city, to become the capital of the Negev. Beersheba now houses the Arid Zones Research Center, a modern hospital and medical school, a theater and concert hall, an archaeological and ethnic museum, as well as housing projects of modern architecture with special consideration for the desert conditions. To complete the picture of the desert capital, a Beduin market convenes every Thursday, where among sheep and camels bargains are struck in the traditional manner after prolonged deliberations.

Traveling southeast along the modern Beersheba–Dead Sea highway, a magnificent range of color and rock formations unfolds—to be interrupted by an incongruous sight: a board informing the traveler that he has reached the sea level, from which he will keep descending to the "bottom of the world", the Dead Sea, 1200 feet below.

twenty, won a war. Suddenly, those men, who not only knew how to die but to die with guns in their hands, became brothers. Better still, they fell on the field of honor for a fatherland. Nothing anymore set them apart from others and they were applauded. For the last hundred years all the great minds in the world have condemned national borders. This is the moment the Jews chose to set up theirs in the most explosive corner of the globe. For the last hundred years those same great minds have condemned wars. This is the moment the Jews chose to carry off their military victory. Hats off to them! In this absurd world they finally decided to play the absurd game common to mankind. At last! Everyone breathed more easily, including the Jew.

The metamorphosis began about one hundred years ago with the mystic desire for a return to Jerusalem.

The evolution half-opened the doors of the ghettos. For two thousand years, from father to son, the prayers of Jews were transmitted with this heartrending cry, "If I forget you, O Jerusalem . . ." Two thousand years is im-

The Greek-Orthodox monastery of Karantel, clings precariously to the steep slope of the mountain regarded by tradition as the Hill of the Temptation of Jesus. From the top of the mountain satan "showed him all the kingdoms of the world" which would be his, if only Jesus "fell down and worshipped him" (Matthiew 4:8–9). In the early centuries pious hermits lived their solitary lives in nearby caves, and gathering only for communal prayer formed a laura, to become later a monastery, whose name "Karantel", or Quarantine (forty) marks the forty days Jesus fasted in this place in order to withstand satan's temptation.

Christian pilgrims immerse in the Jordan river in a symbolic act of baptism at the traditional site of Jesus' baptism. The verdant banks of the Jordan river stand out in striking contrast to the sheer wilderness of the plain of Jericho. Here, over the easily passable, shallow fords opposite Jericho, Joshua crossed the Jordan, leading the Children of Israel into the Promised Land. Here, John the Baptist "preached a baptism of repentance" (Mark 1:4), and Jesus too, was baptized by him in the Jordan. A number of Christian shrines commemorate the site, of which the best known is the Greek-Orthodox Monastery of St. John.

The caves (right) opposite Qumran, the main retreat of the Essenes, a Jewish sect in the times of the Second Temple. Here they left stored in earthenware jars their priceless writings, known as the Dead Sea Scrolls, the discovery of which "revolutionized our knowledge of the texts of the Old Testament and of the Jewish background, time and composition, and historical position of the New Testament" (Prof. W. F. Albright). The caves of the Judean desert served later as refuge of the Bar Kochba rebels in their last stand against Rome. Archaeologists aided by volunteers explore one of the caves (below), using in addition to the usual dig tools a mine-detector, for the possible presence of coins or copper vessels buried in the earth.

Several fresh water springs enliven the arid, salty wilderness of the Dead Sea area. One of these, the Ein Bokek spring, supplies fresh water to the hotels put up by the Dead Sea to accommodate the ever-growing numbers of visitors and patients from all over the world, seeking cure at the hot springs of the Dead Sea. The hot sulphuric springs have gained world renown for their curative qualities, bringing relief from a wide range of ailments, mainly arthritic, rheumatic and skin diseases.

pressive, but it's really only one hundred generations. Not a great number took part in the return to Palestine. But in addition to their faith, they brought with them a Western notion of productivity, of a return to the soil, their soil. For them it was not just a question of adoring the Eternal Father in His country, but of bringing life back to the land that had been holy and which the former occupants had abandoned to the desert. Pure folly, of course. Timid agrarian communities were formed, on which the Turkish authorities kept a favorable or unfavorable eye, but always a lazy one.

And suddenly that *Aliyah*, that "ascent," took form in 1896 when a Vienese journalist, Theodore Herzl, putting black on white, clarified the situation by publishing *The Jewish State*. He commended the colonization of ancient Palestine by the Jews, the word being used in the sense of the development of the soil. The idea excited a large number of Jews for reasons that were no longer religious. Governments became interested in the movement: this could be a solution to the "Jewish problem." "The sick

One of the fresh water sources in the Judean desert, Ein Gedi (the Spring of the Kid), streaming along its stony river bed into the Dead Sea, was named the Brook of David. Here, David the shepherd found refuge from the wrath of King Saul, who sent to seek him out "in the wilderness of Engedi, . . . in front of the Wildgoats' Rock" (I Sam. 24:1–2). The lovely brook sparkling in the wild gorge, foams over the rocks in a charming waterfall, which, surrounded by lush tropical vegetation, is a favorite haunt of picknickers. The Ein Gedi kibutz standing on the banks of the stream, uses part of its waters to irrigate its banana plantations and luscious vegetable gardens—a fascinating sight in the barren salty wilderness by the Dead Sea. The whole area is now a nature reserve, and the graceful ibex (wild mountain goat) with their magnificent curved horns, can often be seen outlined on the steep cliffs above Ein Gedi.

The Dead Sea, at the lowest spot on the surface of the earth, 1,292 feet below sea level. No fish can live in the Dead Sea, since the enormous quantity of minerals (over 25%) contained in its waters destroys practically all organic life. The bitter pungent taste of the water is due to the chloride of magnesium, while the chloride of calcium makes it smooth and oily to the touch. The extremely high specific gravity of the Dead Sea water enables bathers to float freely on its surface, making bathing in this saline lake a unique experience.

Exquisite formations of mineral sediment on the shores of the Dead Sea. The high concentration of alluvial deposits in the waters of the lake, and the enormous evaporation at this lowest-on-earth spot are the artists responsible for this unique décor.

man of Europe," the Ottoman Empire, was shrinking with the passing years; a Western bridgehead was certainly not to be disdained. Utopia or reality, *The Jewish State* gave body to what had formerly been only nostalgia and poetry: "If I forget you, O Jerusalem . . ." A mystical conception emerged: Zionism, coming from the name of one of the hills of the Holy City. Jewish financial circles opened their coffers wide. The plan was of archaic simplicity. With the money collected they would purchase the land from the *effendim*, the owners, who were doing nothing with it. And afterwards install volunteers equipped after a fashion. The Turks had no objection. In comparison with the inflexibility of the Western world, one can even say they were rather understanding.

At the beginning of the twentieth century the Jews of the Aliyah had a stroke of genius, the long-range importance of which they probably did not even realize: they invented the *kibbutz*. It seemed of little importance when Deganya was founded. Weary of the pettiness around them, transported by a thirst for an ideal which could not be measured in

126

Massada, rising about 1000 feet above the shores of the Dead Sea. Surrounded by deep gullies, with steep, almost perpendicular cliffs in the south, east and north, the rock was of a strategically ideal defensive position. Regarding it as a place of last refuge in case of need, Herod the Great transformed the lonely rock into a magnificent fortress, provided with a sumptuous palace (at the pointed northern end), two smaller palace-like structures, storehouses, administrative building, a large public bath of the hypocaust type, and a synagogue facing Jerusalem. A large cistern cut in the top of the rock was part of the ingenious water system which provided water supply to the fortress. Surrounding the whole flat surface of Massada, on the brink of its precipitous sides, stood a casemate wall with guard towers. Occupied at the beginning of the Great Revolt (66–70) by the Zealots, this almost impregnable fortress withstood two and half years of siege after the fall of Jerusalem, and was the last stronghold to hold out against the Romans.

money, a few pioneers decided to organize a small society with a community of interests in which personal property would not exist, where each individual would work for the whole. Others followed the example. An obscure existence dedicated to labor began for those people.

It is certainly not in these few lines that the difficulties encountered can be described. Even Galilee was lacking in everything. Furthermore, the Jewish Agency that served as promoter and intermediary had to be very economical with the funds collected. It was far from rich. The Arabs were often hostile toward the newcomers who were upsetting their habits. The Turkish authorities began to be on their guard. Numerous were the Jews the world over whose generous donations were then distributed by the Jewish National Fund, but many others protested that such a campaign might well awaken dormant anti-Semitism.

Such polemics did not interest the kibbutzim settlers. They removed stones from the land, carried water bucket by bucket, sowed and reaped, ate meagerly, slept on hard beds

129

The western side of the Massada fortress. Here, on the still visible "White Rock" (*leuke*) the Romans built their siege dam rising up the fortress. On this dam they rolled up their siege tower provided with a battering ram, which breached the wall of the fortress. From that moment on it became clear to the defenders that Massada was doomed. When the Romans sure of their victory retreated for the night, the Zealots decided their fate. Encouraged by their leader, Eleazar Ben Yair, rather than become slaves of the Romans, they killed their wives and children and "then chose ten men by lot out of them, to slay all the rest . . . The dead were nine hundred and sixty in number" (Josephus, Wars of the Jews).

Herod's palace at the pointed north end of Massada was built in three tiers. On the topmost level was the dwelling quarter with a semi-circular terrace in front of it. Below, on the middle level, a colonnaded rotunda, and on the lowest level (below) a banqueting hall decorated, like the whole complex, with stuccoed columns topped by Corinthian and Ionian capitals, floors paved with mosaics of geometrical design and walls painted to imitate marble. From here the king could enjoy the magnificent sweeping view of an incomparable composition of color: the golden-brown of the Judean desert, the brilliant blue of the Dead Sea and across it, in the background, the delicate pastel hues of the Moab mountains.

and got up at dawn to resume their back-breaking labor.

The First World War was to bring about an important change in the situation. During military operations, the English drove the Turks from Palestine and, once the hostilities were ended, obtained from the international courts a mandate for the territory. By the Balfour Declaration, Great Britain undertook to create a National Jewish Home in Palestine. Utopia, the old dream of return to the ancestral land had become official reality. But the jubilation was short-lived.

The *effendim* had become aroused: they had sold wasteland and suddenly those stony and arid hills were producing! Financial injuries never being fatal, this could have been settled peacefully. But the Jews were importing farming methods and theories of democratic equality which were endangering the feudal structure of society by destroying the resigned attitude of the people. Arab leaders set the Bedouins against the newcomers. The nomads liked nothing better than to raid the only nearby oases. The British Foreign Office found this extremely irksome.

They appeased the most demanding. The newly created kingdom of Transjordan—which was to become Jordan—found itself excluded from the Mandate. Emigration formalities were tightened to stem the flow. The Jewish Agency was offered territories in Africa where complications seemed temporarily less likely. The Jews turned a deaf ear. Without the appeal which Palestine had for them, how could they ask the pioneers to make the inhuman sacrifices they had accepted? They had even imposed on themselves the revival of a dead language: Hebrew. Zionism was a modern movement: it intoxicated, transported, gave strength to move mountains. These people, composed for the most part of atheists but whose sole bond was religious, suddenly discovered a tradition and clung to it.

Hitlerian Germany poured oil on the fire, courting the Arabs to woo them away from the Union Jack. In reply, London published its White Paper which set an annual limit of 75,000 Jews authorized to return to their so-called National Home. Discontent prevailed. One especially grave consequence of

Flocks of sheep and goats going out to "pasture"—in search of the scanty, barely visible desert vegetation on which these hardy breeds subsist. Sheep and goats are the desert dweller's main source of livelihood and highly prized possessions: the bigger the flock the richer its owner. They constitute also the dowry of the Beduin woman, who from the tenderest age begins her career of shepherdess. The little girl receives from her father several lambs and kids, which reared and bred into a flock will remain, as an economic security, her exclusive property even after her marriage.

the new immigration restrictions aroused indignation: hundreds of thousands of Jews whom Nazism had compelled to flee, and whom no nation wanted, found themselves condemned to death.

Europe, shaken by constant German demands, made half-hearted protests. The only manifestations against this betrayal of the British Mandate took place in the British parliament: both the Conservatives and Labor spoke out energetically against the White Paper. The government paid no heed. And in any case, after the Second World War, Conservatives and Labor alike, when they came into power, maintained the same position as their predecessors.

In Palestine no one was happy with the provision. The Arabs thought it was insufficient. The Jews knew what their co-religionists were enduring elsewhere, and the immigration by driblets was slowing down the accomplishment of the Zionist dream. Sometimes they reacted violently. An undercurrent of anger, of rebellion, had existed since the mandatory powers had allowed whole communities to be massacred. The farmers de-

"The Pillars of Solomon"—huge multi-colored rock formation near the Timna copper mines—owe their name to King Solomon's mines and smelting ovens in the vicinity. Heaps of black slag mark the ancient smelting pits, where the copper was turned into bronze—the highly prized metal of antiquity.

manded arms to defend their villages. They were refused. As for official help in the event of attack, it always arrived too late. Those men and women were willing to die, were willing to be defeated, but not without fighting for their cause. Enough of resignation, enough of compromise. The Jewish State so long desired had to be deserved, had to be won. The right to live meant nothing; sweat had no market value, neither unjustly shed blood. Those around them respected only strength: they would be strong. Politically speaking, this new trend took the form of *revisionism*; practically speaking, the clandestine importation of arms and munitions. Jewish opinion in Palestine was divided. Some still believed in forbearance and patience at all costs: the majority. However, a minority had confidence in action alone, violent action and, if need be, terrorism.

The two groups agreed on one point—to bring in secretly as many refugees as possible.

1939–1945: a forced truce. The Palestinian Jews fought on the British side; the Arabs openly bet on an Axis victory. With the return of peace this was perhaps what induced the English to maintain the restrictions in the White Paper. Such proof of friendship would surely assure them of Arab goodwill, even if the horror-stricken world was learning of the extent of the Jewish holocaust: six million human beings burned in crematoriums; even if the immigration restrictions affected the rare survivors of the concentration camps; even if it meant the slow stifling of half a million allies, henceforth prisoners in Palestine.

On the one hand, 600,000 men, women, children and old people organized the clandestine entrance of the unfortunate homeless seeking refuge. On the other, the Royal Navy guarded the Mediterranean coast. The Jewish world redoubled its efforts and offerings. For fabulous prices they bought old tubs ready for the scrap-heap, which carried full cargoes of exhausted, suffering flesh. Visitors to Israel can still see on the road between Tel-Aviv and Haifa the old hulls which ran the British blockade. Indifferent to universal censure, the British intercepted the "illegals," imprisoning behind barbed wires the survivors of the death camps.

The "Ships of the Desert" getting ready for a lengthy crossing. The ungainly appearance of these animals is deceptive: their agility and speed in the sandy wastes is unmatched, their silent swinging gait amazingly graceful. The supercilious haughty look belies their shyness, and the lovely long-lashed primadonna eyes are strangely matched with the ugly faces of these fascinating beasts. Their long memory is proverbial: they will keep a grudge for years against someone who has harmed them, and remind him of it at the first opportunity with a rather unpleasant nip of their huge grinding teeth. Eminently adapted to harsh desert conditions, their water supply stored in their humps to last them for several days, these hardy animals subsist on thorny bushes which not even the tough all-eating goats would deign to touch. Camels are the Beduin's most prized possession as beast of burden and means of transport as well as livelihood.

Beduin encampment in the Negev. Since immemorial times, these nomadic tribes have wandered with their flocks in search of pasture the rocky wilderness and sandy wastes of the Middle Eastern deserts. Their social structure, mores and traditions are a fascinating reflection of the lifestyle prevalent in the times of the Patriarchs. But times are changing for the Beduin too: all the children of the Israeli Beduin now attend elementary schools, some proceed to secondary schools and universities. The Beduins learned to appreciate the comforts of permanent habitation too and have established with Government help attractive villages, where their womenfolk enjoy the unheard-of luxury: plumbing, running water and electricity. The tractor has replaced the wooden plough, and the motor vehicle the camel—wherever possible. But the lure of the desert, its freedom and wild beauty still hold their enchanting spell on some of these "sons of the desert".

An oasis near Eilat. This is the northernmost point where these Sudanese palms grow. Their sweet delicious fruit is the favorite staple food of the desert dweller, the Beduin.

Zionism became resistance. While negotiating with the U.N. and Great Britain, it armed the *Haganah*, the Jewish fighting force organized by the British and dissolved by them when they no longer needed it. Perhaps mankind, emerging from the most murderous war in history, might never have taken any notice of those half-million men who, for the thousandth time in two thousand years, demanded their due: a place in the sun. However, among the combatants a few impassioned men attracted attention. Dangerous madmen. Exasperated madmen who said that it was not enough to ward off blows or to "match" them—a knock-out was needed. Take the offensive. Talking is not enough, talk the loudest. A few thousand, no more, who furthermore were not in complete agreement, formed two groups of determined militants, of desperados, both hunted by the British police and condemned by their compatriots. The task undertaken was so disproportionate, the deeds accomplished reflected such sublime bravery, that the world suddenly became aware and was moved. Without those terrorists, the extraordinary

141

The glory of the "silent world" in the Red Sea (left). The marvelous hues of the Red Sea landscape pale into insignificance before the unrivaled magnificence of color and breathtaking beauty hidden beneath the luminous surface: coral reefs of most wondrous variety of pattern studded with spiky, black sea-urchins, scarlet sea-anemones, teeming with tropical fish, whose diversity of shape and brilliance of coloring depass imagination. The coast of Eilat (below) with its modern elegant hotels and lovely lagoon is a favorite of vacationers—Israeli as well as tourists from all over the world. Eilat on the Red Sea is the most southern town and harbor of Israel, its gateway to the African continent and to the Far East.

Traveling south along the coast of the Red Sea is an unforgettable experience. A magnificent range of color unfolds in the ever-changing scenery: the subdued pastels of yellow, brown and purple of the majestic mountains of Sinai, offset by glorious hues of brilliant azure, sapphire and violet of the sea. One of the outstanding beauty spots along this coast is the "fjord", its waters teeming with most brilliantly colored tropical fish.

uprising of the Warsaw ghetto might well have been forgotten. Comparisons were made with David and Goliath. In Ramat Gan a monument was erected to the memory of Dov Gruner, one of the resistants, twenty years old and hanged by the British. It depicts a lion cub attacking the British lion.

The secret Haganah, while safeguarding an appearance of lawfulness, the Stern and Irgun groups, other smaller units and isolated individuals, all stood fast during the years following the armistice of May, 1945. To add the last straw to the reactions aroused by the spectacular attacks, catastrophes occurred, bringing their crushing weight of dead. The *Struma*, loaded to overflowing with miserable "illegals," was lost with all hands in the Black Sea. One survivor out of 764 passengers. The *Patria*, stopped by the Royal Navy, blew up in the bay of Haifa — 250 useless deaths out of 1800 refugees. The tale of the *Exodus* was added to all this. Almost everywhere people began to take David's side. Goliath, disgusted, gave up his mandate.

144

St. Catherine Monastery at the foot of Jebel Musa, the "Mount of Moses" in southern Sinai. An early Christian tradition points out this mountain as the site where Moses received the Tablets of the Law with the Ten Commandments. A small chapel on the peak of the 6,600 feet high mountain commemorates the event of Lawgiving. Another tradition believed the foot of the mountain to be the site of the "burning bush", from which God first spoke to Moses. Drawn in early times to these sites of God's revelation hermits and anchorites formed here a laura, at an altitude of 4,500 feet above sea level. In the 4th century Constantine the Great erected on the site a chapel and a tower where the hermits could find refuge in times of danger. But the number of the monks grew and the tower could no longer provide adequate protection from marauding nomads, so in the 6th century emperor Justinian I constructed around it a fortress-like monastery for them, enclosing it within high granite walls. The entire complex is today essentially as it was built by Justinian. The monastery was named after Catherine, a Christian saint, who was martyred in Alexandria in the 4th century. Left, the chapel and other structures inside the St. Catherine monastery compound.

The British soldiers reembarked in orderly fashion. The last was scarcely aboard before, in a house in Tel-Aviv, a handful of responsible men proclaimed the creation of the Jewish State, advocated half a century before by an inspired writer, Theodore Herzl. Jerusalem has erected a mausoleum in his memory.

But Israel, that day, had no time to celebrate or rejoice. Those 600,000 refugees from nowhere were living in the midst of a million Arabs not at all inclined to let them do so. The tiny newborn state was encircled by Egypt, Jordan, Lebanon and Syria who had sworn to wipe off the map the name Israel which as yet scarcely existed. While independence was being declared, a wave of allied Arabs swept over the country; in every city the Arabs attacked the Jews. David and Goliath again.

Emissaries traveled the world over to buy arms and ship them back. Secretly, of course, for virtue reigns everywhere and no one was going to encourage a war, after all! The Arabs had everything they needed, it's true, but they were normally constituted states

Serabit el-Khaddem, in Sinai, the remains of the temple of the goddess Hathor, the "Lady of the Turquoise". The goddess was the patroness of the turquoise quarries nearby, from which the lovely semi-precious stones so highly valued in ancient Egypt were extracted by Semitic slaves, from which the name *Serabit el-Khaddem* derives its name: the "Lookout of the Slaves". The temple dates from the 4th millenium B.C. and was composed of different parts which were added by successive Egyptian pharaohs, each vying to outdo his predecessor in magnificence of construction. Hieroglyphic inscriptions carved in the obelisque-like stones still standing or strewn about on the site tell the stories and give records of the numerous Egyptian expeditions to the turquoise mines.

which had placed their orders in peacetime.

In Europe and in America people were getting ready to go into mourning, to shed sincere tears for the first and last independent Jews in our civilization. However, the unbelievable happened: Israel drove out the invader. The Arab defeat very nearly allowed the new state to get its bearings, but others stepped in, eager to put an end to the whole thing, and imposed a hasty truce. Since then, the Arabs have refused to discuss peace terms.

The unbelievable again occurred despite logical predictions. Brand new, unsteady, strangled, surrounded by enemies, obliged to maintain an army on a permanent war footing, Israel settled down on its narrow couch, affirmed its vitality, grew and multiplied. Israel existed.

What is it that half a million travelers seek in Israel each year? Many things. One arrives with definite ideas: Christian or Jewish pilgrimages, a historical-archeological voyage, sun, sports, rest. There is, however, such a variety of material that it's tempting to browse in other fields. Nothing prevents

The rugged mountain ranges in southern Sinai of red and
grey granite interspersed with black dikes, rising to a height
of nearly 8,000 feet, are one of the earliest mountain formations on earth. They present a view of majestic wild beauty,
grandiose and primitive as they must have looked at the
hour of Creation.

Christ's followers, or the "Gentile members"
of the Mediterranean Vacation Club, or the
Hassids "made in U.S.A.", from going a bit
out of their way to Elath to see for themselves
that the bottom of the Red Sea really is covered with coral, or to visit thirty-odd layers
of civilizations superimposed in the former
fortress of Megiddo. The desert, the Dead
Sea, Acre, Nazareth, Tiberias, Jerusalem
lavish their treasures indiscriminately on all
comers.

Of course, you say, but there are as many
other excursion sites in other countries.

That extra something which Israel offers
is the miracle—recent, contemporary, present, daily.

Here is an example: between Jerusalem
and Beersheba an experiment has been made
since 1955. A number of villages were set up,
the new settlers aiming to engage in agricul-
ture. They are grouped around a main town—
also new—responsible for collecting and dis-
tributing the produce, for furnishing raw ma-
terials, equipment, tools, as well as being the
administrative backbone of the ensemble.
The villages, according to the settlement

plan, were to be the active members of this new body and the town would carry out the function of the heart and lungs. This is the Lakisch region—the city is Kiryath-Gat.

Now, a strange phenomenon took place here. The locality was not suited for tourist trade: the government did not encourage it for it could hamper eventual troop movements on the edge of the desert; the road from Ashkelon was bad, virtually unfit for travel; the one between Jerusalem and Beersheba was used only by motorists in a hurry to reach their destination; finally, from the touristic point of view there is very little to see. And yet people stop at Kiryath-Gat and show very marked interest and curiosity. The tourist, since we must call him by his name, the traveler, alert and organized, breaks instinctively with the tradition which demands that he take interest only in things of the past. Suddenly the present and the future become fascinating. Here lies Israel's charm for the foreigner: the human adventure—contemporary, current, real—fires his interest, sometimes without him even being aware of it.

In his "Pensées" Pascal said, "The Jews stand on the middle ground between the Christians and the pagans: the Christians know the true God and do not love the earth; the pagans do not know God and love only the earth; the Jews know the true God and they love the earth."

Four hundred in Abraham's wake, 600,000 in 1948, approximately 3,500,000 now, 15% of which are minorities. For an exhausted population, exsanguine from their trials, this last increase represents one immigrant to welcome *every 5 minutes*, to feed, lodge, instruct, and put to work.

Figures speak but they don't satisfy. Twenty-eight years to provide the best-intentioned Gentiles—those who distinguish politely between Jews and Israelites ("Ah! If only all Jews were like you!")—with a new distinction between Israelites and Israelis.

Whatever one may pretend to the contrary, we have not lost the admiration for military and national virtues. The *sabra,* who with his bare hands blew up an enemy tank, has acquired a glory comparable to that of the three men who, in one century, have revolutionized the social, philosophical, and scientific conceptions of the planet: Marx, Freud, Einstein, which is just another paradox. Old La Fontaine did his best, but the image of the uprooted oak, its haughty and fatal inflexibility appears far more noble to us than the reed which yields but does not break.

In the tulmult of ovations, our heroes' principal title to glory was passed over in silence. Whereas the Jew has for so long been called a greedy shopkeeper and usurer, the Israeli seems unquestionably to be the most selfless man on earth. Between members of the kibbutzim and moshavim—that other form of collective society—employees in cooperatives earning the same salary, researchers who, by definition, scorn profit, civil servants who, without a murmur, receive less pay than our streetcleaners, and soldiers who earn virtually nothing, we arrive at a proportion of 20% to 25% of the population who have chosen to earn their living instead of money.

No one shirks work. And let there be no mistake: the competition in Israel is terrible; the day's activities begin at 7 a.m. The leisurely and lazy should not apply.

Naturally, the picture is not all rosy; in Jerusalem and Tel Aviv profiteers are not lacking. But at least they too know why they are working, and they too believe, and have proved it, that the common interest is more important than personal gain. This "naiveté" is their saving grace; elsewhere it would be their downfall.

The fairy tales of our childhood ended with, "They were married and lived happily ever after." Israel's history, as of 1948, could be summed up in the same fashion, "They proclaimed their independence and set to work."

They are not "out of the woods" yet, far from it. But they say, "In our country whoever does not believe in miracles is not realistic."

ILLUSTRATIONS

MILESTONES IN THE HISTORY OF ISRAEL

BC 1850	Abraham leaves Ur in Chaldea at God's command.
1600 (ca.)	Joseph establishes his father in Gossen in Egypt. Beginning of the slavery which will last 300, 400, or 600 years.
1250–1200	Led by Moses, the Hebrews leave Egypt en route for the Promised Land.
1230 (ca.)	The revelation at Mount Sinai.
1200–1180	Joshua's conquest of the Promised Land.
1110	Victory of Israel (the prophetess Deborah) over the Canaanites.
1050	Defeat of Israel at Aphek. Loss of the Ark of the Covenant. (The Philistines will return it to make peace and David will bring it to Jerusalem, dancing before it.)
1020	Saul, Israel's first king, dies at Gilboa. David's reign begins.
1000	David, king of Israel, makes an alliance with Hiram, king of Phoenicia.
970	Construction of the Temple of Jerusalem under Solomon, known henceforth as the First Temple.
933	Schism of the ten tribes. Kingdoms of Israel and Judah.
890	Elijah the Prophet.
850	The alliance of Israel and Judah against Mesha, king of Moab. The Mesha steles—*first texts dated with certainty*.
721	Fall of Samaria, the capital of the kingdom of Israel conquered by Salmanesser and Sargon, Assyrian kings.
700–600	Assyrian attempts to conquer Judah. The star of Babylon rises again; the fall of Nineveh. The prophets Isaiah, Jeremiah, Habakkuk. Nebuchadnezzar, king of Babylon.
589	Nebuchadnezzar sacks Jerusalem and destroys the Temple.
587–538	Captivity in Babylon. King Cyrus of Persia conquers Babylon and authorizes the Jews to rebuild Jerusalem and their Temple.
515	Completed, the new Temple of Jerusalem is dedicated, to be known henceforth as the Second Temple.
332	Alexander the Great of Macedonia conquers the Persians but dies in the campaign. The vast holdings are divided by his generals who establish two dynasties of Hellenistic rule:

Ptolemies in Egypt and Seleucides in Syria. Beginning of the Hellenistic period.

198 Judaea under the Seleucides. Enforcement of Hellenistic culture and interference with religious worship cause friction between the Jews and the Greeks.

169–167 Revolt of the Hasmoneans (Maccabees) following repeated desecrations of the Temple.

166–63 The Hasmonean dynasty. Territorial expansion, introduction of a wide system of education, the emergence of the Pharisaic schools of Oral Law.

63 The appearance of Rome on the scene. Jerusalem falls into the hands of Pompey: beginning of Roman occupation.

37 Herod the Great, King of Judaea. His reign is marked by prosperity, building projects of fortresses and cities on a vast scale and architectural excellence.

0 Birth of Jesus.

33 Crucifixion of Jesus.

66–70 The Great Revolt of the Jews against the Romans.

70 (Aug. 10) Titus sacks Jerusalem and sets fire to the Temple. First dispersion of the Jewish people.

132–135 The second revolt against the Romans, led by Bar Kochba and rabbi Akiba. Jerusalem razed, the site turned into Aelia Capitolina and forbidden to the Jews. Second dispersion of the Jewish people.

135–1917 *Diaspora.*

586–601 The Visigothic king of Spain orders compulsory baptism for everyone, pagans and Jews included.

626 The "good king" Dagobert expels the Jews from France.

1095 The Council of Clermont proclaims the Crusade against the Infidels; official beginning of persecution.

1120–1198 Averröes in Spain. He writes: "Humanity has been seduced by three impostors: Moses, Jesus Christ and Mohammed. The Eucharist makes the Christian religion an impossible religion. The multiplicity of precepts makes Judaism a puerile religion. The limitation of pleasure condems Islam to be only a religion of swine." No measures are taken against him.

1139–1209 Maimonides in Spain about whom Casaubon declares, "He is the first rabbi who has

157

stopped writing a lot of twaddle." He is obliged to flee.

1144	First trial for ritual murder, led by a convert, Theobald of Cambridge.
1160–1173	Benjamin of Tudela travels extensively in the Middle East. The present inhabitants of Tudela (Spain) are unaware that this Jew has made their name famous; and even that there was once a Jewish quarter in their city.
1181	Philippe-August levies a special tax on the Jews.
1187	Saladin defeats the Crusaders in the Holy Land. Jerusalem returns to Moslem rule and Jews begin to return to the City.
1242	Saint Louis presides over the burning of sacred Jewish books.
1247	Trial for ritual murder in Valréas (County of Avignon).
1264	Boleslaw of Kalish in Poland establishes a relatively liberal law for the Jews.
1290	Expulsion of the Jews from England.
1348	Epidemic of the black death, the plague. Jews are burned everywhere; 2,000 in Strasbourg.
1361	The burning at the stake in Chinon are more modest: 160 Jews.
1394	Expulsion of the Jews from France.
1399	Poznan pogrom.
1406	Cracow pogrom.
1480	In Muscovy—where Jews are not admitted—the slaughter of Judaizing Christians.
1492	The discovery of America; total victory over Islam. Expulsion of the Jews from Spain (approx. one million). The rise and intensification of the Inquisition in Spain and all over Europe. Some Spanish and Italian Jews reach Palestine and settle mainly in the four holy cities: Jerusalem, Hebron, Safed and Tiberias.
1563	Capture of Polotsk by Ivan the Terrible: all Jews are drowned in the Dvina River.
1648	Revolt of the Ukrainian Cossacks under Chmielnicki, accompanied by pogroms in which perished over 200,000 Jews.
	In Smyrna, Turkey, Sabbetai Zvi claims to be the Messiah. His disciples, the *deunmés*, still live in Turkey (Moslem Jews).
1649	Cromwell decrees the admission of Jews into England.

1632–1677	Baruch Spinoza.
1760	Death of the *Besht* (Baal Shem Tov), founder of *Hassidism*.
1768–1772	First division of Poland: a million Jews taken over by Russia. New Cossack uprising accompanied by pogroms in which 70,000 Jews perished.
1782	Joseph II of Austria publishes the Edict of Tolerance.
1789	Declaration of the Rights of Man. Abbot Grégoire in the Constituant Assembly says, "50,000 Frenchmen (Jews) are going to sleep tonight as serfs; act in such a way that they will wake up free citizens tomorrow."
1791	Death of Jacob Frank, who continued and adapted the teachings of Sabbetai Zvi, in Germany. The *Frankists* (Christian Jews) still exist.
1816–1883	Karl Marx.
1827	Tsar Nicholas I establishes compulsory military service of 25 years for the Jews.
1850–1939	Sigmund Freud.
1860	First Jewish settlement outside the city walls of Jerusalem.
1861	By abolishing serfdom Tsar Alexander II betters the condition of the Russian Jews.
1879–1955	Albert Einstein.
1881–1900	Beginning of the "Return to the Land" movement. Jewish pioneers from Russia, the *Biluim*, establish the first agricultural settlements in the Holy Land: Rishon le-Zion, Nes Ziona, Zikhron Ya'acov, Gadera, Rehovot etc.
1892	Trial for ritual murder in Xanthen, Germany.
1894–1906	The "regrettable" Dreyfus Affair in France.
1896	Publication of *The Jewish State* by Theodore Herzl, the father of political Zionism. (The precursors: Hess, Ahad-Ha'am, Kalisher, Alkalay, Pinsker).
1900	Trial for ritual murder in Konitz. Jewish immigration into Palestine gathers momentum. More agricultural settlements are established.
1909	The establishment of Tel-Aviv on the sand dunes by the Mediterranean.
1917	The British under general Allenby wrest Palestine from the Turks.
1917–1919	In the period following the Russian Revolution during the Civil War over 100,000 Jews

	(civilians) massacred by the warring parties in the Ukraine.
1922	The League of Nations gives a mandate to Great Britain for the establishment of a Jewish National Home in Palestine, and for "encouraging Jewish immigration" (Art. 6).
1939	Publication of the British "White Paper" making official all the restrictions previously employed against Jewish immigration, bitterly resented and opposed by the 500,000 Palestinian Jews.
1939–1945	A truce in Palestine due to World War II. Genocide in Europe.
1945–1948	"Illegal" immigration fights its way into Palestine through the blockade of the British Navy. Jewish resistance intensifies: the underground fighters of the Haganah, Irgun, and Lehi challenge the British Empire, forcing it to return the Mandate.
1947	The United Nations adopt a resolution of partition of Palestine into a Jewish and Arab states, with internationalization of Jerusalem. The resolution is accepted by the Jews and rejected by the Arabs.
1948	The British leave Palestine. The Jews proclaim the independent Jewish State of Israel. Five neighboring Arab states invade the newborn State and are defeated. An armistice follows.
1956	The Sinai Campaign secures free passage of Israeli shipping through the Straits of Tiran, the entrance to the Red Sea.
1958	First international Bible contest.
1960	Discovery of Bar Kochba's letters in the Judean desert. Completion of an atomic reactor in Israel.
1967	The closure of the Straits of Tiran by Egypt and the continual harassment of the border settlements by Syria and Egypt precipitates the Six Day War. Jordan enters the war by bombarding the western (Israeli) part of Jerusalem, resulting in the re-unification of Jerusalem, as the capital of the State of Israel.
1973	The combined Egyptian-Syrian surprise attack on Israel, the *Yom Kippur* (Day of Atonement) War to put an end to the Jewish state, ends with their defeat, at the cost of thousands of precious lives to both sides.